GOURMET BURGERS

Publications International, Ltd.

Pictured on the front cover *(left to right, row 1)*: Backyard Barbecue Burgers (*page 59*), Cubano Burgers (*page 19*), Aloha Burgers with Pineapple Chutney (*page 31*); (*row 2*) Spicy Cheeseburger Sliders (*page 135*), Gourmet Burgers with Pancetta and Gorgonzola (*page 47*), Portobello Mushroom Burger with Mozzarella (*page 127*); (*row 3*) Great Grilled Burgers with Spinach Pesto (*page 5*), Two-Bite Burgers (*page* 151), and Veggie-Packed Turkey Burgers (*page 101*).

Pictured on the back cover *(left to right)*: Cheddar-Beer Burgers with Bacon (page 53), Buffalo Sliders (*page 159*), and Grilled Potato Salad (*page 165*).

ISBN: 978-1-68022-506-8

Library of Congress Control Number: 2016936144

Manufactured in China.

8 7 6 5 4 3 2 1

Microwave Cooking: Microwave ovens vary in wattage. Use the cooking times as guidelines and check for doneness before adding more time.

Preparation/Cooking Times: Preparation times are based on the approximate amount of time required to assemble the recipe before cooking, baking, chilling or serving. These times include preparation steps such as measuring, chopping and mixing. The fact that some preparations and cooking can be done simultaneously is taken into account. Preparation of optional ingredients and serving suggestions is not included.

Publications International, Ltd.

TABLE OF CONTENTS

BEEF & BEYOND

GREAT GRILLED BURGERS WITH SPINACH PESTO

MAKES 4 SERVINGS

Spinach Pesto (recipe follows)

1½ pounds ground beef

¼ teaspoon salt

¼ teaspoon black pepper

4 to 8 slices provolone cheese

4 crusty Italian rolls, cut in half and toasted

4 to 8 slices tomatoes

Oak leaf lettuce

1 Prepare Spinach Pesto. Prepare grill for direct cooking.

2 Combine beef, ¼ cup pesto, salt and pepper in large bowl; mix lightly. Shape into 4 patties about ¾ inch thick. Reserve remaining pesto.

3 Place patties on grid over medium heat. Grill, covered, 8 to 10 minutes (or uncovered, 13 to 15 minutes) to medium (160°F) or to desired doneness, turning occasionally. Top each burger with cheese during last 2 minutes of grilling.

4 Spread remaining pesto on cut sides of each roll. Top bottom half of each roll with burger, tomato, lettuce and top half of roll.

SPINACH PESTO

Combine 2 cups spinach leaves, 3 tablespoons grated Romano cheese, 3 tablespoons olive oil, 1 tablespoon dried basil, 1 tablespoon lemon juice and 3 cloves garlic in food processor or blender. Process until smooth. Makes about ½ cup.

4

POLYNESIAN BURGERS

MAKES 6 SERVINGS | PREP TIME 10 MINUTES **COOK TIME** 20 MINUTES

1½ pounds ground beef

1 can (8 ounces) pineapple slices in juice, undrained

1 can (10½ ounces) CAMPBELL'S® Condensed French Onion Soup

2 teaspoons packed brown sugar

1 tablespoon cider vinegar

1 loaf French bread, cut crosswise into 6 pieces

1 Shape the beef into **6** (½-inch-thick) burgers.

2 Cook the burgers in a 12-inch skillet over medium-high heat until well browned on both sides. Pour off any fat. Top **each** burger with **1** slice pineapple. Reserve the pineapple juice.

3 Stir the soup, reserved pineapple juice, brown sugar and vinegar in a small bowl. Add the soup mixture to the skillet and heat to a boil. Reduce the heat to low. Cover and cook for 5 minutes or until the burgers are cooked through.

4 Split the bread pieces. Serve the burgers and sauce on the bread.

SPICY ONION BURGERS

MAKES 6 SERVINGS | PREP TIME 10 MINUTES **GRILL TIME** 10 MINUTES

1½ pounds ground beef

½ cup PACE® Picante Sauce

1 envelope (about 1 ounce) dry onion soup and recipe mix

6 PEPPERIDGE FARM® Classic Sandwich Buns with Sesame Seeds

Lettuce leaves

Tomato slices

Avocado slices

1 Mix **thoroughly** the beef, picante sauce and soup mix. Shape **firmly** into **6** burgers, ½-inch thick **each**.

2 Lightly oil the grill rack and heat the grill to medium. Grill the burgers for 10 minutes or until desired doneness, turning the burgers over halfway through grilling.

3 Serve on buns with lettuce, tomato, avocado and additional picante sauce.

BEEF BURGERS WITH CORN SALSA

MAKES 4 SERVINGS

½ cup frozen corn

½ cup peeled seeded chopped tomato

1 can (about 4 ounces) diced green chiles, divided

1 tablespoon chopped fresh cilantro *or* 1 teaspoon dried cilantro

1 tablespoon white vinegar

1 teaspoon olive oil

¼ cup fine dry bread crumbs

3 tablespoons milk

¼ teaspoon garlic powder

12 ounces 95% lean ground beef

Lettuce leaves

1 Prepare corn according to package directions; drain. Combine corn, tomato, 2 tablespoons chiles, cilantro, vinegar and oil in small bowl. Cover and refrigerate until ready to serve.

2 Preheat broiler. Combine bread crumbs, remaining chiles, milk and garlic powder in medium bowl. Add beef; mix lightly. Shape mixture into 4 (¾-inch-thick) patties. Place on broiler pan.

3 Broil patties 4 inches from heat 6 to 8 minutes. Turn and broil 6 to 8 minutes or until cooked through (160°F). Serve on lettuce leaves; spoon salsa over burgers.

CLASSIC CALIFORNIA BURGERS

MAKES 4 SERVINGS | PREP TIME 10 MINUTES **COOK TIME** 10 MINUTES

2 tablespoons FRENCH'S® Honey Dijon Mustard

2 tablespoons mayonnaise

2 tablespoons sour cream

1 pound ground beef

2 tablespoons FRENCH'S® Worcestershire Sauce

1⅓ cups FRENCH'S® Cheddar or Original French Fried Onions, divided

½ teaspoon garlic salt

¼ teaspoon ground black pepper

4 hamburger rolls, split and toasted

½ small avocado, sliced

½ cup sprouts

1 Combine mustard, mayonnaise and sour cream; set aside.

2 Combine beef, Worcestershire, ⅔ cup French Fried Onions and seasonings. Form into 4 patties. Grill over high heat until juices run clear (160°F internal temperature).

3 Place burgers on rolls. Top each with mustard sauce, avocado slices, sprouts and remaining onions, dividing evenly. Cover with top halves of rolls.

BBQ CHEESE BURGERS

Top each burger with 1 slice American cheese, 1 tablespoon barbecue sauce and 2 tablespoons French Fried Onions.

PIZZA BURGERS

Top each burger with pizza sauce, mozzarella cheese and French Fried Onions.

BACON AND BLUE CHEESE STUFFED BURGERS

MAKES 4 SERVINGS

4 slices applewood-smoked bacon
  or regular bacon

1 small red onion, finely chopped

2 tablespoons crumbled blue
  cheese

1 tablespoon butter, softened

1½ pounds ground beef
  Salt and black pepper

4 onion or plain hamburger rolls
  Lettuce leaves

---

1 Cook bacon in large skillet over medium-high heat until almost crisp. Remove to paper towels to drain; finely chop bacon. Place in small bowl. Add onion to same skillet; cook and stir 5 minutes or until soft. Add to bowl with bacon. Cool slightly. Stir in blue cheese and butter until well blended.

2 Prepare grill for direct cooking.

3 Divide ground beef into 8 equal portions. Flatten into thin patties about 4 inches wide; season with salt and pepper. Place 2 tablespoons bacon mixture in center of each of 4 patties; cover with remaining patties and pinch edges together to seal.

4 Grill patties, covered, over medium-high heat 8 to 10 minutes (or uncovered 13 to 15 minutes) for medium doneness (160°F), turning once. Transfer burgers to platter; let stand 2 minutes before serving. Serve burgers on rolls with lettuce.

TIP

If you want juicy, flavorful burgers, do not flatten the patties. Pressing down on the patties with a spatula not only squeezes out tasty juices, but in this recipe it might also cause the stuffing to pop out.

EAST MEETS WEST BURGERS

MAKES 4 SERVINGS | PREP AND COOK TIME 30 TO 40 MINUTES

- 1 pound Ground Beef (95% lean)
- ¼ cup soft whole wheat bread crumbs
- 1 large egg white
- ¼ teaspoon salt
- ⅛ teaspoon black pepper
- 4 whole wheat hamburger buns, split

SESAME-SOY MAYONNAISE

- ¼ cup light mayonnaise
- 1 tablespoon thinly sliced green onion, green part only

- ½ teaspoon soy sauce
- ¼ teaspoon dark sesame oil
- ⅛ teaspoon ground red pepper

SLAW TOPPING

- ½ cup romaine lettuce, thinly sliced
- ¼ cup shredded red cabbage
- ¼ cup shredded carrot
- 1 teaspoon rice vinegar
- 1 teaspoon vegetable oil
- ¼ teaspoon black pepper

1 Combine Sesame-Soy Mayonnaise ingredients in small bowl; refrigerate until ready to use. Combine Slaw Topping ingredients in small bowl; set aside.

2 Combine Ground Beef, bread crumbs, egg white, salt and ⅛ teaspoon black pepper in large bowl, mixing lightly but thoroughly. Lightly shape into four ½-inch-thick patties.

3 Place patties on grid over medium, ash-covered coals. Grill, covered, 11 to 13 minutes (over medium heat on preheated gas grill, covered, 7 to 8 minutes) until instant-read thermometer inserted horizontally into center registers 160°F, turning occasionally. About 2 minutes before burgers are done, place buns, cut sides down, on grid. Grill until lightly toasted.

4 Spread equal amount of Sesame-Soy Mayonnaise on bottom of each bun; top with burger. Evenly divide Slaw Topping over burgers. Close sandwiches.

COOK'S TIPS

To make soft bread crumbs, place torn bread in food processor or blender container. Cover; process, pulsing on and off, to form fine crumbs. One and one-half slices makes about 1 cup crumbs.

Cooking times are for fresh or thoroughly thawed ground beef. Color is not a reliable indicator of ground beef doneness.

courtesy The Beef Checkoff

CUBANO BURGERS

MAKES 4 SERVINGS

1½ pounds ground pork

¼ cup minced green onions

3 tablespoons yellow mustard, divided

1 tablespoon minced garlic

2 teaspoons paprika

½ teaspoon black pepper

¼ teaspoon salt

8 slices Swiss cheese

4 bolillos or Kaiser rolls, split and toasted

8 slices sandwich-style dill pickles

¼ pound thinly sliced ham

1 Prepare grill for direct cooking.

2 Combine pork, green onions, 1 tablespoon mustard, garlic, paprika, pepper and salt in large bowl; mix lightly but thoroughly. Shape into 4 patties about ¾ inch thick, shaping to fit rolls.

3 Place patties on grid over medium heat. Grill, covered, 8 to 10 minutes (or uncovered, 13 to 15 minutes) or until cooked through (160°F), turning occasionally. Top each burger with 2 slices Swiss cheese during last 2 minutes of grilling.

4 Spread remaining 2 tablespoons mustard over cut sides of rolls. Place pickles on bottom half of each roll. Top each with burger and ham. Cover with top halves of rolls. Press down firmly.

NOTE

Traditional Cuban sandwiches are made with sliced roast pork and do not include mayonnaise, tomatoes, onions, bell peppers or lettuce. Thinly sliced plantain chips usually accompany the sandwiches.

SUBSTITUTION

A bolillo is an oval shaped roll about 6 inches long with a crunchy crust and a soft inside. If you can't find bolillos, use a loaf of French bread. Cut in half and then into individual-sized portions.

BBQ BURGERS WITH COLESLAW

MAKES 4 SERVINGS | PREP TIME 35 MINUTES

¼ cup light sour cream

1 teaspoon sugar

1 teaspoon apple cider vinegar

¼ teaspoon dry mustard

¼ teaspoon garlic powder

2 cups DOLE® Classic Cole Slaw

Salt and black pepper

Paprika

1¼ pounds ground beef

½ cup prepared barbecue sauce, divided

4 sesame seed hamburger buns, split

- Mix sour cream, sugar, vinegar, mustard and garlic powder. Toss with cole slaw blend; season with salt, pepper and paprika to taste.

- Mix meat with 2 tablespoons barbecue sauce; season with salt and pepper. Form meat into 4½-inch patties. Grill over medium-high heat, brushing frequently with barbecue sauce, 5 to 6 minutes on each side or until cooked to desired temperature. Toast the buns, cut side down, just before serving.

- Place patty on bottom half of each bun. Top with ½ cup coleslaw and other half of bun. Serve with roasted potato wedges.

PINEAPPLE VARIATION

Add ½ cup diced fresh DOLE® Tropical Gold® pineapple.

WESTERN BARBECUE BURGERS WITH BEER BARBECUE SAUCE

MAKES 4 SERVINGS

1½ pounds ground beef

1 cup smokehouse-style barbecue sauce

¼ cup brown ale

½ teaspoon salt

¼ teaspoon black pepper

1 red onion, cut into ½-inch-thick slices

4 hamburger buns

8 slices thick-cut bacon, crisp-cooked

Lettuce leaves

Tomato slices

1 Prepare grill for direct cooking over medium-high heat. Shape beef into 4 patties about ¾ inch thick.

2 Combine barbecue sauce, ale, salt and pepper in small saucepan. Bring to a boil; boil 1 minute. Set aside.

3 Grill burgers, covered, 8 to 10 minutes or to desired doneness, turning occasionally. Grill onion 4 minutes or until softened and slightly charred, turning occasionally.

4 Serve burgers on buns topped with onion, bacon, barbecue sauce mixture, lettuce and tomatoes.

ITALIAN BURGERS WITH OLIVES & MOZZARELLA

MAKES 6 SERVINGS | PREP TIME 10 MINUTES **COOK TIME** 25 MINUTES

1½ pounds ground beef

1 can (10¾ ounces) CAMPBELL'S® Condensed Tomato Soup

⅓ cup water

½ teaspoon dried oregano leaves, crushed

⅓ cup sliced pimento-stuffed olives

6 slices mozzarella cheese **or** provolone cheese

12 slices Italian bread

1 Shape the beef into **6** (½-inch thick) burgers.

2 Cook the burgers in a 12-inch skillet over medium-high heat until well browned on both sides. Pour off any fat.

3 Stir the soup, water, oregano and olives in the skillet and heat to a boil. Reduce the heat to low. Cover and cook for 5 minutes or until desired doneness.

4 Top the burgers with the cheese and cook until the cheese is melted. Serve the burgers on the bread with the soup mixture for dipping.

THAI BURGER

MAKES 4 SERVINGS

1 pound Ground Beef

1 cup shredded Napa cabbage

2 tablespoons fresh lime juice, divided

½ cup chopped green onions

1 teaspoon ground ginger

1 teaspoon hot chili sauce

1 tablespoon creamy peanut butter

1 tablespoon hoisin sauce

1 teaspoon toasted sesame oil

Salt and pepper

4 whole wheat or white hamburger buns, split

1 Combine cabbage and 1 tablespoon lime juice in medium bowl; set aside.

2 Combine Ground Beef, green onions, ground ginger and hot sauce in medium bowl, mixing lightly but thoroughly. Lightly shape into four ½-inch thick patties.

3 Heat nonstick skillet over medium heat until hot. Place patties in skillet; cook 10 to 12 minutes until instant-read thermometer inserted horizontally into center registers 160°F, turning occasionally. Season with salt and pepper, as desired.

4 Meanwhile, combine peanut butter, hoisin sauce, remaining 1 tablespoon lime juice and sesame oil in small bowl. Cover and refrigerate until ready to use.

5 Place 1 burger on bottom half of each bun; top evenly with peanut butter mixture and cabbage mixture. Close sandwiches.

COOK'S TIPS

Hot chili sauce, an Asian condiment made from red chilies, garlic and vinegar, imparts a tangy, spicy heat to dishes. Hot chili sauce is available in Asian markets and the Asian section of most supermarkets.

Cooking times are for fresh or thoroughly thawed Ground Beef. Color is not a reliable indicator of Ground Beef doneness.

Four large Napa cabbage leaves may be substituted for hamburger buns. Drizzle cabbage leaves with lime juice and set aside until burgers are ready to be served. Continue as directed in step 5, omitting shredded cabbage and serving burgers in cabbage leaves.

courtesy The Beef Checkoff

SALSA BACON BURGERS WITH GUACAMOLE

MAKES 4 BURGERS | PREP TIME 10 MINUTES **START TO FINISH** 25 MINUTES

1 pound ground beef

1 packet (1.25 ounces) ORTEGA®
   Taco Seasoning Mix

¼ cup ORTEGA® Salsa, any variety

2 ripe avocados

1 packet (1 ounce) ORTEGA®
   Guacamole Seasoning Mix

4 hamburger buns

8 slices cooked bacon

COMBINE ground beef, taco seasoning mix and salsa in large mixing bowl. With clean hands, form meat mixture into 4 patties.

CUT avocados in half and remove pits. Scoop out avocado meat and smash in small bowl. Add guacamole seasoning mix. Set aside.

HEAT large skillet over medium heat; cook burgers 5 minutes. Flip burgers and continue to cook another 7 minutes.

PLACE burgers on bottom of buns. Top each burger with dollop of guacamole, 2 slices bacon and top bun.

TIP

Make burgers half the size to create great sliders.

ALOHA BURGERS WITH PINEAPPLE CHUTNEY

MAKES 6 SERVINGS

- 2 tablespoons butter
- 2 tablespoons packed dark brown sugar
- ¼ cup cola beverage
- ¼ cup balsamic vinegar
- ½ medium red onion, diced
- 1 small tomato, seeded and diced
- 1½ cups diced pineapple
- 2 pounds ground beef

- 2 tablespoons teriyaki sauce
- 2 teaspoons Worcestershire sauce
- 2 teaspoons onion powder
- 1½ teaspoons salt
- 2 teaspoons black pepper
  Additional salt and black pepper
- 6 brioche buns,* toasted

*If unavailable, substitute hamburger buns.

1 Melt butter in medium saucepan over medium-low heat; stir in brown sugar until blended. Stir in cola and vinegar; bring to a boil. Reduce heat to low; simmer 20 minutes, stirring frequently.

2 Stir in onion; cook and stir 2 minutes on medium heat. Add tomato and pineapple, stir to coat and turn off heat.

3 Combine beef, teriyaki sauce, Worcestershire sauce, onion powder, 1½ teaspoons salt and 2 teaspoons pepper in medium bowl; mix lightly. Shape into 6 patties.

4 Meanwhile, cook burgers under broiler or on grill pan over medium-high heat, 6 minutes on each side. When cooked to desired doneness, keep warm. Return pineapple mixture to high heat and cook 1 minute. Season with salt and pepper. Top each burger with a heaping spoonful of pineapple mixture. Serve on toasted brioche buns.

GREEK LAMB BURGERS

MAKES 4 SERVINGS

¼ cup pine nuts

1 pound ground lamb

¼ cup finely chopped yellow onion

3 cloves garlic, minced and divided

¾ teaspoon salt

¼ teaspoon black pepper

¼ cup plain yogurt

¼ teaspoon sugar

4 slices red onion (¼ inch thick)

1 tablespoon olive oil

8 pumpernickel bread slices

12 thin cucumber slices

4 tomato slices

1 Spread pine nuts in small skillet. Cook over medium heat 1 to 2 minutes or until nuts are lightly browned, stirring frequently.

2 Prepare grill for direct cooking. Oil grid. Combine lamb, pine nuts, yellow onion, 2 cloves garlic, salt and pepper in large bowl; mix well. Shape mixture into 4 patties about ½ inch thick and 4 inches in diameter. Combine yogurt, sugar and remaining 1 clove garlic in small bowl; mix well.

3 Brush one side of each patty and red onion slice with oil; place on grid, oiled sides down. Brush tops with oil. Grill over medium-high heat, covered, 8 to 10 minutes to medium (160°F) or to desired doneness, turning halfway through grilling time. Grill bread 1 to 2 minutes per side during last few minutes of grilling.

4 Serve patties on bread with red onion, tomato, cucumber and yogurt mixture.

HAWAIIAN-STYLE BURGERS

MAKES 6 SERVINGS

1½ pounds ground beef

⅓ cup chopped green onions

2 tablespoons Worcestershire
sauce

⅛ teaspoon black pepper

⅓ cup pineapple preserves

⅓ cup barbecue sauce

6 pineapple slices

6 hamburger buns, split and
toasted

1 Combine beef, green onions, Worcestershire sauce and pepper in large bowl.
Shape into 6 (½-inch-thick) patties.

2 Combine preserves and barbecue sauce in small saucepan. Bring to a boil over
medium heat, stirring often.

3 Spray grid with nonstick cooking spray. Prepare grill for direct cooking. Place
patties on grid over medium coals. Grill, covered, 8 to 10 minutes (or uncovered,
13 to 15 minutes) to medium (160°F), turning and brushing often with sauce.
Place pineapple on grid; grill 1 minute or until browned, turning once.

4 To serve, place patties and pineapple on buns.

BROILING DIRECTIONS

Arrange patties on rack in broiler pan. Broil 4 inches from heat until cooked
through (160°F), turning and brushing often with sauce. Broil pineapple 1 minute,
turning once.

SUPER PORK BURGER

MAKES 6 SERVINGS | PREP TIME 15 MINUTES **COOK TIME** 15 MINUTES

1 (8-ounce) can crushed pineapple

¾ pound fully cooked boneless smoked ham

¾ pound ground pork

½ cup finely chopped green bell pepper

2 tablespoons all-purpose flour

¼ teaspoon ground allspice

1 Drain pineapple, reserving juice.

2 Coarsely chop ham. Place ham in food processor bowl; process about 30 seconds or until coarsely ground.

3 In mixing bowl, combine pineapple, ground ham, ground pork, bell pepper, flour and allspice; mix well. Shape into six ½-inch-thick patties. Place patties on unheated rack in broiler pan. Broil 6 inches from heat about 8 minutes.

4 Meanwhile, in small saucepan cook pineapple juice over medium heat until reduced by half. Brush patties with half of pineapple juice; turn and broil 6 minutes longer. Brush patties with remaining pineapple juice.

courtesy National Pork Board

GRILLED MAUI BURGERS

MAKES 4 SERVINGS | PREP TIME 15 MINUTES **GRILL TIME** 15 MINUTES

1 can (8 ounces) pineapple slices in juice, drained (4 slices)

1 cup PACE® Picante Sauce

1 pound lean ground beef

4 slices deli Monterey Jack cheese (about 3 ounces)

4 PEPPERIDGE FARM® Classic Hamburger Buns, split and toasted

½ avocado, peeled, pitted and cut into 4 slices

1   Lightly oil the grill rack and heat the grill to medium. Grill the pineapple for 5 minutes or until tender, turning it over once halfway through the grill time. Remove the pineapple to a cutting board. Dice the pineapple. Stir the pineapple and **⅔ cup** picante sauce in a medium bowl.

2   Thoroughly mix the beef and the remaining picante sauce in a large bowl. Shape the beef mixture into **4** (½-inch-thick) burgers.

3   Grill the burgers for 10 minutes for medium or until desired doneness, turning the burgers over once halfway through the grill time. Top the burgers with the cheese.

4   Serve the burgers on the buns. Top with the pineapple-picante mixture and the avocado.

MEDITERRANEAN BURGERS

MAKES 4 SERVINGS

1½ pounds ground beef

2 tablespoons grated Parmesan cheese

2 tablespoons chopped kalamata olives

1 tablespoon chopped fresh parsley

1 tablespoon diced tomato

2 teaspoons dried oregano

1 teaspoon black pepper

4 slices mozzarella cheese

4 hamburger buns, split

1 Prepare grill for direct cooking.

2 Combine beef, Parmesan cheese, olives, parsley, tomato, oregano and pepper in medium bowl; mix lightly. Shape into 4 (½-inch-thick) patties.

3 Grill patties over medium heat, covered, 8 to 10 minutes (or uncovered, 13 or 15 minutes) to medium (160°F) or to desired doneness, turning halfway through grilling. Top each burger with 1 slice mozzarella cheese just before removing to bun.

SERVING SUGGESTION

For even more Mediterranean-inspired flavor, thinly slice bottled roasted red peppers and add to burgers to taste.

AUDACIOUS TWO-CHEESE BURGERS

MAKES 4 SERVINGS

1½ pounds ground beef

⅓ cup chopped fresh parsley

1 tablespoon Dijon mustard

1 tablespoon Worcestershire sauce

¾ teaspoon black pepper, divided

½ teaspoon dried thyme

½ thinly sliced English cucumber

3 slices red onion, separated into rings

4 radishes, thinly sliced

1 tablespoon olive oil

1 teaspoon red wine vinegar

¼ teaspoon salt

4 slices Cheddar cheese

4 slices Gouda cheese

4 leaves green leaf lettuce

4 whole wheat rolls, split and toasted

Ketchup

1 Prepare grill for direct cooking. Combine beef, parsley, mustard, Worcestershire sauce, ½ teaspoon pepper and thyme in large bowl; mix lightly. Shape into 4 patties about ¾ inch thick. Cover and refrigerate.

2 Combine cucumber, onion, radishes, oil, vinegar, salt and remaining ¼ teaspoon pepper in small bowl; mix well.

3 Place patties on grid over medium heat. Grill, covered, 8 to 10 minutes (or uncovered, 13 to 15 minutes) to medium (160°F) or to desired doneness, turning halfway through grilling time. Top burgers with Cheddar cheese during last 2 minutes of grilling.

4 Place 1 slice Gouda cheese on bottom half of each roll; top with cucumber mixture, lettuce and burgers. Spread ketchup on top half of each roll; place on burgers.

BRIE BURGERS WITH SUN-DRIED TOMATO AND ARTICHOKE SPREAD

MAKES 4 SERVINGS

1 cup canned quartered artichokes, drained and chopped

½ cup oil-packed sun-dried tomatoes, drained and chopped, divided

2 tablespoons mayonnaise

1 tablespoon plus 1 teaspoon minced garlic, divided

1 teaspoon black pepper, divided

½ teaspoon salt, divided

1½ pounds ground beef

¼ cup chopped shallots

¼ pound Brie cheese, sliced

2 tablespoons butter, softened

4 egg or Kaiser rolls, split

Heirloom tomato slices

Arugula or lettuce leaves

1 Prepare grill for direct cooking.

2 Combine artichokes, ¼ cup sun-dried tomatoes, mayonnaise, 1 teaspoon garlic, ½ teaspoon pepper and ¼ teaspoon salt in small bowl; mix well.

3 Combine beef, shallots, remaining ¼ cup sun-dried tomatoes, 1 tablespoon garlic, ½ teaspoon pepper and ¼ teaspoon salt in large bowl; mix lightly. Shape into 4 patties.

4 Grill over medium heat, covered, 8 to 10 minutes (or uncovered, 13 to 15 minutes) or until cooked through (160°F), turning occasionally. Top each burger with cheese during last 2 minutes of grilling.

5 Spread butter on cut surfaces of rolls; grill or toast until lightly browned. Spread artichoke mixture on bottom halves of rolls. Top with tomato slice, burger and arugula. Cover with top halves of rolls.

GOURMET BURGERS WITH PANCETTA AND GORGONZOLA

MAKES 4 SERVINGS

1½ pounds ground beef

1 cup (4 ounces) gorgonzola or blue cheese crumbles

2 tablespoons mayonnaise

1 red bell pepper, quartered

4 thick slices red onion

Salt and black pepper

4 egg or brioche rolls, split and toasted

Oak leaf or baby romaine lettuce

4 to 8 slices pancetta or bacon, crisp-cooked

1 Prepare grill for direct cooking. Shape beef into 4 patties about ¾ inch thick. Cover and refrigerate. Combine cheese and mayonnaise in small bowl; refrigerate until ready to serve.

2 Grill bell pepper and onion, covered, over medium-high heat 8 to 10 minutes or until browned, turning once. (Use grill basket, if desired.) Transfer to plate; keep warm.

3 Place patties on grid over medium heat. Grill, covered, 8 to 10 minutes (or uncovered, 13 to 15 minutes) to medium (160°F) or to desired doneness, turning occasionally. Season with salt and black pepper.

4 Spread cheese mixture on cut surfaces of rolls. Top bottom half of each roll with lettuce, burger, pancetta, onion, bell pepper and top half of roll.

DELUXE MEDITERRANEAN LAMB BURGERS

MAKES 4 SERVINGS

1½ pounds ground lamb

1 tablespoon minced garlic

2 teaspoons Greek seasoning

1 teaspoon paprika

½ teaspoon salt, divided

½ teaspoon black pepper

4 thin slices red onion, separated into rings

1 tablespoon olive oil

1 teaspoon chopped fresh mint *or* parsley

1 teaspoon red wine vinegar

Spinach leaves

4 whole grain rolls, split and toasted

4 to 8 slices tomatoes

1 package (4 ounces) feta cheese crumbles or Mediterranean feta cheese crumbles

1 Prepare grill for direct cooking.

2 Combine lamb, garlic, Greek seasoning, paprika, ¼ teaspoon salt and pepper in large bowl; mix lightly but thoroughly. Shape into 4 patties about ¾ inch thick. Cover and refrigerate.

3 Combine onion, oil, mint, vinegar and remaining ¼ teaspoon salt in small bowl; toss to coat.

4 Place patties on grid over medium heat. Grill, covered, 8 to 10 minutes (or uncovered, 13 to 15 minutes) to medium (160°F) or to desired doneness, turning occasionally.

5 Place spinach on bottom halves of rolls. Top with burgers, tomatoes, onion mixture and feta cheese. Cover with top halves of rolls.

DELUXE BACON & GOUDA BURGERS

MAKES 4 SERVINGS

1½ pounds ground beef

⅓ cup mayonnaise

1 teaspoon minced garlic

¼ teaspoon Dijon mustard

2 thick slices red onion

Salt and black pepper

4 to 8 slices Gouda cheese

Butter lettuce leaves

4 onion rolls, split and toasted

Tomato slices

4 to 8 slices bacon, crisp-cooked

1 Prepare grill for direct cooking. Shape beef into 4 patties about ¾ inch thick. Cover and refrigerate. Combine mayonnaise, garlic and mustard in small bowl; mix well. Set aside.

2 Grill patties and onion over medium-high heat, covered, 8 to 10 minutes (or uncovered, 13 to 15 minutes) until cooked through (160°F) or to desired doneness, turning occasionally. Remove onion when slightly browned. Season burgers with salt and pepper. Top with cheese during last 2 minutes of grilling.

3 Place lettuce on bottom half of each roll; top with mayonnaise mixture, burger, tomato, onion, bacon and top half of roll.

SUBSTITUTION

Use a prepared mayonnaise spread for the garlic mayonnaise.

CHEDDAR-BEER BURGERS WITH BACON

MAKES 4 SERVINGS

1½ pounds lean ground beef

4 ounces sharp Cheddar cheese, cut into ½-inch cubes

½ cup beer

¼ cup chopped fresh parsley

1 teaspoon paprika

¾ teaspoon garlic powder

¾ teaspoon salt

¼ teaspoon black pepper

¼ cup ketchup

2 tablespoons mayonnaise

4 hamburger buns

4 lettuce leaves

4 slices tomato

4 thick slices red onion

8 slices bacon, cooked

1 Prepare grill for direct cooking over medium-high heat.

2 Combine beef, cheese, beer, parsley, paprika, garlic powder, salt and pepper in large bowl; stir to blend. Shape into 4 patties, making centers of patties slightly thinner than edges.

3 Grill patties, covered, 8 to 10 minutes (or uncovered, 13 to 15 minutes) to medium (160°F) or to desired doneness, turning once.

4 Meanwhile, combine ketchup and mayonnaise in small bowl. Top bottom half of each bun with 1½ tablespoons ketchup mixture, lettuce leaf, tomato slice, onion slice, burger and 2 bacon slices; cover with top halves of buns.

SWEDISH "MEATBALL" BURGERS

MAKES 6 SERVINGS

3 tablespoons butter, divided

1 small onion, chopped

¼ cup milk

2 packages (3 ounces each) ramen noodles, any flavor, crushed*

1 egg

1 teaspoon salt, divided

½ teaspoon black pepper, divided

¼ teaspoon ground allspice

1½ pounds ground beef

¼ cup all-purpose flour

1 can (about 14 ounces) beef broth

½ cup whipping cream

Hard rolls

Cranberry sauce (optional)

Discard seasoning packets.

1   Melt 2 tablespoons butter in medium saucepan over medium heat. Add onion; cook 3 minutes or until translucent. Reduce heat to medium-low; add milk. Bring to a simmer. Add crushed noodles; remove from heat.

2   Whisk egg, ½ teaspoon salt, ¼ teaspoon pepper and allspice in large bowl. Add noodle mixture; stir to combine. Add beef; stir until well blended. Shape into 6 patties.

3   Preheat broiler. Broil burgers on rack 4 inches from heat 10 minutes until medium rare (145°F), or desired doneness.

4   Melt remaining 1 tablespoon butter in saucepan. Add flour; cook 2 to 3 minutes or until lightly browned, whisking constantly. Gradually whisk in broth and cream. Bring to a boil; cook 2 minutes or until thickened. Stir in remaining salt and pepper.

5   Serve burgers on rolls with cream sauce and cranberry sauce, if desired.

ULTIMATE GRILLED BURGERS

MAKES 4 SERVINGS

1½ pounds boneless beef chuck, excess fat trimmed, cut into 1½-inch chunks

1½ teaspoons kosher salt *or* 1¼ teaspoons regular salt

½ teaspoon black pepper

Canola or olive oil, for brushing

4 hamburger buns, split

Sliced tomatoes, lettuce leaves, raw red onion rings and pickle slices

Assorted condiments, such as tomato ketchup, mayonnaise and mustard

---

1 Spread beef chunks on baking sheet. Freeze until semi-frozen and firm, about 1 hour.

2 Fit stand mixer with food grinder and coarse blade. Grind meat into medium bowl. Add salt and pepper and mix with clean hands. Do not overmix. Shape into 4 (4-inch-diameter) patties, making 1-inch wide shallow indentation in center of each patty to discourage shrinkage. Cover with plastic wrap and let stand while grill heats (not longer than 1 hour). Preheat grill to high.

3 Lightly brush patties with oil. Place on grill and cover. Grill 2½ minutes or until browned on bottom. Turn and grill until other sides are browned and meat still feels soft when pressed in center with finger, about 2½ minutes more for medium-rare. If flare-ups occur, move to outer edge of charcoal grill (not over coals) or a turned-off area of gas grill. Transfer to plate. Add buns to grill, cut sides down, and grill until toasted, about 1 minute. Add to plate with burgers.

4 Serve immediately with desired toppings and condiments.

BACKYARD BARBECUE BURGERS

MAKES 6 SERVINGS

1½ pounds ground beef

⅓ cup barbecue sauce, divided

1 onion, cut into thick slices

1 tomato, sliced

2 tablespoons olive oil

6 Kaiser rolls, split

6 leaves green or red leaf lettuce

1 Prepare grill for direct cooking. Combine beef and 2 tablespoons barbecue sauce in large bowl. Shape into 6 (1-inch-thick) patties.

2 Grill patties, covered, over medium heat 8 to 10 minutes (or uncovered, 13 to 15 minutes) to medium (160°F) or to desired doneness, turning occasionally. Brush both sides with remaining barbecue sauce during last 5 minutes of cooking.

3 Meanwhile, brush onion* and tomato slices with oil. Grill onion slices about 10 minutes and tomato slices 2 to 3 minutes.

4 Just before serving, place rolls, cut side down, on grid; grill until lightly toasted. Serve burgers on rolls with tomato, onion and lettuce.

Onion slices may be cooked on the stovetop. Heat 2 tablespoons oil in large skillet over medium heat; add onions and cook 10 minutes or until tender and slightly browned, stirring frequently.

ZESTY BLUE CHEESE BURGERS

MAKES 4 SERVINGS | PREP TIME 15 MINUTES **COOK TIME** 15 MINUTES

½ cup HEINZ® Tomato Ketchup

½ cup crumbled blue cheese

2 tablespoons finely chopped onion

1 tablespoon LEA & PERRINS® Worcestershire Sauce

1 pound lean ground beef

4 sandwich buns, split and toasted

1 To prepare sauce, combine Ketchup, blue cheese, onion and Worcestershire Sauce.

2 Lightly mix ¼ cup sauce with meat; shape into four patties.

3 Grill or broil to desired doneness.

4 Serve in toasted buns topped with remaining sauce.

CURRIED BEEF BURGERS

MAKES 4 SERVINGS

1 pound 95% lean ground beef

¼ cup mango chutney, chopped

¼ cup grated apple

1½ teaspoons curry powder

½ teaspoon salt

⅛ teaspoon black pepper

1 large red onion, cut into ¼-inch slices

Lettuce leaves

1 large tomato, sliced

4 Kaiser rolls or hamburger buns

1 Prepare grill for direct cooking. Combine beef, chutney, apple, curry powder, salt and pepper in medium bowl; mix lightly. Shape into 4 patties.

2 Grill over medium heat, covered, 8 to 10 minutes (or uncovered, 13 to 15 minutes) or until cooked through (160°F), turning once. Grill onion 5 minutes or until lightly charred, turning once. Place lettuce on bottom halves of rolls. Top with burgers, tomato, onion and top halves of rolls.

BISTRO ONION BURGERS

MAKES 6 SERVINGS | PREP TIME 5 MINUTES **COOK TIME** 10 MINUTES

1½ pounds ground beef

1 envelope (about 1 ounce) dry onion soup and recipe mix

3 tablespoons water

6 PEPPERIDGE FARM® Classic Sandwich Buns with Sesame Seeds, split and toasted

Lettuce leaves

Tomato slices

1 Thoroughly mix the beef, soup mix and water. Shape the beef mixture into **6** (½-inch-thick) burgers.

2 Cook the burgers in batches in a 10-inch skillet over medium-high heat until well browned on both sides, 10 minutes for medium or to desired doneness.

3 Serve the burgers on the buns. Top with the lettuce and tomato.

BACON BURGERS

MAKES 4 SERVINGS

8 slices bacon, crisp-cooked and divided

4 pounds ground beef

1½ teaspoons chopped fresh thyme *or* ½ teaspoon dried thyme

½ teaspoon salt

Dash black pepper

4 slices Swiss cheese

1 Prepare grill for direct cooking. Crumble 4 slices bacon.

2 Combine beef, crumbled bacon, thyme, salt and pepper in medium bowl; mix lightly. Shape into 4 patties.

3 Grill patties over medium-high heat, covered, 8 to 10 minutes (or uncovered, 13 to 15 minutes) until cooked through (160°F) or to desired doneness, turning occasionally. Top with cheese during last 2 minutes of grilling. Serve with remaining bacon slices.

BLUE CHEESE BURGERS

MAKES 4 SERVINGS

1¼ pounds ground beef

1 tablespoon finely chopped onion

1½ teaspoons chopped fresh thyme *or* ½ teaspoon dried thyme

¾ teaspoon salt

Dash black pepper

4 ounces blue cheese, crumbled

Dijon mustard (optional)

4 whole wheat hamburger buns

Lettuce leaves

Tomato slices

1 Prepare grill for direct cooking.

2 Combine beef, onion, thyme, salt and pepper in medium bowl; mix lightly. Shape into 8 patties.

3 Place cheese in center of 4 patties to within ½ inch of outer edge; top with remaining patties. Press edges together to seal.

4 Grill over medium heat, covered, 8 to 10 minutes (or uncovered, 13 to 15 minutes) or until cooked through (160°F), turning once. Spread mustard on bottom halves of buns, if desired. Top with lettuce, tomatoes, burgers and top halves of buns.

GRILLED REUBEN BURGER

MAKES 6 SERVINGS

1½ pounds ground beef

½ cup water

½ cup shredded Swiss cheese
(about 2 ounces)

1 envelope LIPTON® RECIPE
SECRETS® Onion Soup Mix*

1 tablespoon crisp-cooked
crumbled bacon or bacon bits

½ teaspoon caraway seeds
(optional)

*Also terrific with LIPTON® RECIPE
SECRETS® Onion Mushroom Soup Mix.*

1 In large bowl, combine all ingredients; shape into 6 patties.

2 Grill or broil until done. Top, if desired, with heated sauerkraut and
additional bacon.

LIPTON® ONION BURGERS

MAKES 8 SERVINGS | PREP TIME 10 MINUTES **COOK TIME** 12 MINUTES

1 envelope LIPTON® RECIPE
SECRETS® Onion Soup Mix*

2 pounds ground beef

½ cup water

*Also terrific with LIPTON® RECIPE
SECRETS® Beefy Onion, Onion Mushroom,
or Savory Herb with Garlic Soup Mix.*

1 In large bowl, combine all ingredients; shape into 8 patties.

2 Grill or broil until done.

BLACK & BLUE BURGERS

MAKES 4 SERVINGS

1 package (16 ounces) JOHNSONVILLE® Bratwurst Patties

1 can (2.25 ounces) sliced black olives, drained

¾ cup crumbled bleu cheese

4 Kaiser rolls, split

2 tablespoons butter

1 Preheat grill to medium-low. Grill patties according to package directions. Top each patty with olives and bleu cheese. Cover and grill until cheese is melted.

2 Grill rolls for 1 to 2 minutes or until lightly toasted. Butter the rolls; top with patties.

RAGÚ® PIZZA BURGERS

MAKES 6 SERVINGS | PREP TIME 10 MINUTES **COOK TIME** 15 MINUTES

1 pound ground beef

2 cups RAGÚ® Old World Style®
  Pasta Sauce, divided

1 cup shredded mozzarella cheese
  (about 4 ounces), divided

¼ teaspoon salt

6 English muffins, split and
  toasted

1 In small bowl, combine ground beef, ½ cup Pasta Sauce, ½ cup cheese and salt.
  Shape into 6 patties. Grill or broil until done.

2 Meanwhile, heat remaining pasta sauce. To serve, arrange burgers on muffin
  halves. Top with remaining cheese, sauce and muffin halves.

SUPER SIMPLE BLUE CHEESE BURGERS

MAKES 8 SERVINGS

1 envelope WISH-BONE® Super
Creamy Blue Cheese Dressing
& Seasoning Mix

2 pounds lean ground beef

1 Combine WISH-BONE® Super Creamy Blue Cheese Dressing & Seasoning Mix
and ground beef; shape into 8 patties.

2 Grill or broil burgers, turning once, 12 minutes or until done. Arrange burgers on
buns and top with your favorite toppings.

POULTRY PLEASERS

TURKEY BURGERS WITH PESTO-RED PEPPER MAYONNAISE

MAKES 4 SERVINGS | PREP TIME 10 MINUTES **COOK TIME** 8 MINUTES

¼ cup HELLMANN'S® or BEST FOODS® Light Mayonnaise*

1 tablespoon prepared pesto

1 tablespoon finely chopped roasted red pepper

4 turkey burgers

4 Kaiser or whole grain rolls

Tomato slices

Lettuce leaves

Onion slices (optional)

Also terrific with HELLMANN'S® or BEST FOODS® Low Fat Mayonnaise Dressing or Canola Cholesterol Free Mayonnaise.

Combine HELLMANN'S® or BEST FOODS® Light Mayonnaise, pesto and roasted pepper in small bowl; set aside.

Grill or broil turkey burgers 8 minutes or until thoroughly cooked, turning once. To serve, evenly spread Mayonnaise mixture on rolls, then top with burgers, tomato, lettuce, onion and dollop of Mayonnaise mixture.

TIP

To perk up the flavor of your burgers, mix WISH-BONE® Italian Dressing into the ground beef or ground turkey.

STUFFED TURKEY BURGERS WITH SMOKY AÏOLI

MAKES 6 SERVINGS

AÏOLI

- ½ cup 93% fat-free mayonnaise
- 1 canned chipotle pepper in adobo sauce, seeded, minced
- ¾ teaspoon adobo sauce (from can above)
- 1 clove garlic, minced

BURGERS

- 1½ pounds lean ground turkey
- 1 cup QUAKER® Oats (quick or old fashioned, uncooked)
- 3 cloves garlic, minced

- 2 tablespoons Worcestershire sauce
- 1½ teaspoons dried oregano leaves
- 1 teaspoon salt
- ½ teaspoon black pepper
- 6 fresh mozzarella balls (⅓ to ½ ounce each)
- 6 whole-wheat hamburger buns, split and lightly toasted
- ¾ cup jarred roasted red pepper halves, drained
- 1 bunch watercress, arugula or other favorite salad greens, stems removed

---

1 For aïoli, combine mayonnaise, chipotle pepper, adobo sauce and garlic in small bowl; mix well. Chill at least 30 minutes.

2 Heat grill or broiler.

3 For burgers, combine turkey, oats, garlic, Worcestershire sauce, oregano, salt and pepper in large bowl; mix lightly but thoroughly. Shape into 6 large patties, about ¼-inch thick. Place 1 mozzarella ball in center of each patty; shape burger mixture around cheese to completely enclose; reshape into patty.

4 Grill or broil 4 inches from heat 5 minutes on each side or until centers are no longer pink (170°F). Arrange burgers on bottom halves of buns; top with aïoli, roasted pepper pieces, watercress and bun tops.

TIP

If small fresh mozzarella balls are unavailable, substitute large fresh mozzarella balls, cut into ⅓- to ½-ounce pieces. A 3-ounce chunk of part-skim mozzarella cheese, cut into 6 pieces, can be substituted for fresh mozzarella.

MUSHROOM, ONION & PEPPER SMOTHERED BURGERS

MAKES 4 SERVINGS | PREP TIME 15 MINUTES **COOK TIME** 20 MINUTES

- 2 tablespoons I CAN'T BELIEVE IT'S NOT BUTTER!® Light Spread, divided
- 1 container (8 ounces) sliced mushrooms
- 2 medium green, red and/or yellow bell peppers, sliced

- 1 medium onion, thinly sliced
- 1 pound lean ground turkey or beef, shaped into 4 patties
- 4 whole grain Kaiser rolls or hamburger buns, split and toasted

1 Melt 1 tablespoon I CAN'T BELIEVE IT'S NOT BUTTER!® Light Spread in 12-inch nonstick skillet over medium-high heat and cook mushrooms, stirring frequently, 5 minutes or until golden; remove mushrooms from skillet and keep warm.

2 Melt remaining 1 tablespoon Spread in same skillet over medium heat and cook bell peppers with onion, stirring frequently, 10 minutes or until very tender. Add to mushrooms and keep warm.

3 Cook burgers in same skillet over medium-high heat, turning once, 5 minutes or until burgers are thoroughly cooked. Serve on rolls, then top with mushrooms, bell peppers and onion.

TIP

Try using different kinds of mushrooms such as cremini or baby bella.

CHICKEN BURGERS WITH WHITE CHEDDAR

MAKES 4 SERVINGS

1¼ pounds ground chicken

1 cup plain dry bread crumbs

½ cup diced red bell pepper

½ cup ground walnuts

¼ cup sliced green onions

¼ cup light beer

2 tablespoons chopped fresh parsley

2 tablespoons lemon juice

2 cloves garlic, minced

¾ teaspoon salt

⅛ teaspoon black pepper

4 slices white Cheddar cheese

4 whole wheat buns

Dijon mustard and lettuce leaves

---

1 Combine chicken, bread crumbs, bell pepper, walnuts, green onions, beer, parsley, lemon juice, garlic, salt and black pepper in large bowl; mix lightly. Shape into 4 patties.

2 Spray large skillet with nonstick cooking spray; heat over medium-high heat. Cook patties 6 to 7 minutes on each side or until cooked through (165°F). Place cheese on patties; cover skillet just until cheese melts.

3 Serve burgers on buns with mustard and lettuce.

SAVORY CHICKEN BURGERS

MAKES 2 SERVINGS | PREP TIME 12 MINUTES **COOK TIME** 15 MINUTES

2 tablespoons PROMISE® Buttery
Light Spread, divided

1 cup thinly sliced red onion

4 cremini or white mushrooms,
finely chopped (about 1 cup)

1 clove garlic, finely chopped

1 cup firmly packed baby spinach
or arugula

½ pound ground chicken

1 cup finely shredded carrots,
chopped

2 green onions, finely chopped

2 100-calorie whole wheat
sandwich thins

4 cups romaine lettuce, shredded

1 medium tomato, diced

1 cup sliced cucumbers

3 tablespoons WISH-BONE® Light
Italian Dressing

1   Melt 1 tablespoon PROMISE® Buttery Light Spread in 10-inch nonstick skillet
over medium-high heat and cook red onion and mushrooms, stirring
occasionally, 4 minutes or until almost tender. Stir in garlic and cook, stirring
occasionally, 1 minute or until vegetables are tender. Stir in spinach and cook
1 minute or until wilted. Season, if desired, with black pepper. Remove vegetables
from skillet. Reserve half of the vegetable mixture in medium bowl and keep
warm.

2   Combine ground chicken, carrots, green onions and remaining half of the slightly
cooled vegetables in medium bowl; shape into 2 patties.

3   Melt remaining 1 tablespoon Spread in same skillet over medium heat and cook
burgers, turning once, 8 minutes or until chicken is thoroughly cooked. Arrange
burgers on sandwich thins, then top with reserved vegetables.

4   In a bowl, combine lettuce, tomato and cucumbers. Toss with WISH-BONE®
Light Italian Dressing. Serve alongside Chicken Burgers.

TIP

Substitute ground turkey for ground chicken and prepare as above.

SOUTHWEST CHICKEN BURGERS WITH AVOCADO SALAD

MAKES 4 SERVINGS

1 cup finely diced yellow or red bell pepper, divided

½ cup finely diced red onion, divided

1 egg white

1½ teaspoons chili powder, divided

1 pound ground chicken

1 medium avocado, diced

½ cup finely diced cucumber

Juice of 1 lime

4 tablespoons shredded Cheddar cheese

1 Combine ½ cup bell pepper, ¼ cup onion, egg white and 1 teaspoon chili powder in large bowl. Add chicken; stir to combine. Shape mixture into 4 patties. Cover and refrigerate 15 minutes.

2 Combine avocado, cucumber, lime juice, remaining bell pepper, onion and chili powder in medium bowl.

3 Spray large skillet with nonstick cooking spray; heat over medium heat. Cook burgers 5 minutes. Turn and top each burger with 1 tablespoon cheese. Cook 5 minutes or until no longer pink in center.

4 Divide avocado salad among 4 plates; top with cheese-topped burger.

APPLE-KISSED TURKEY BURGERS

MAKES 4 SERVINGS | PREP TIME 15 MINUTES **BROIL TIME** 10 MINUTES **COOK TIME** 5 MINUTES

Butter-flavored vegetable cooking spray

¾ pound ground turkey

½ cup chopped peeled apple

2 green onions, chopped (about ¼ cup)

¾ teaspoon lemon pepper

¼ teaspoon salt

⅛ teaspoon apple pie spice **or** 1 pinch **each** ground cinnamon **and** allspice

½ cup chili sauce

½ cup apple jelly

4 PEPPERIDGE FARM® Hamburger Rolls, split and toasted

1 Heat the broiler. Spray a broiler pan with the cooking spray.

2 Thoroughly mix the turkey, apple, green onions, lemon pepper, salt and apple pie spice in a medium bowl. Shape the turkey mixture into **4** (¾-inch-thick) burgers.

3 Broil the burgers 6 inches from the heat for 10 minutes or until cooked through, turning them over once halfway through the broiling time.

4 Heat the chili sauce and jelly in a 1-quart saucepan over medium heat until the mixture is hot and bubbling, stirring occasionally.

5 Top the burgers with the chili sauce mixture. Serve the burgers on the rolls.

MAKE-AHEAD TIP

The turkey mixture and chili sauce mixture can be prepared a day in advance and refrigerated, tightly covered. Broil the burgers and reheat the sauce just before serving.

CHUTNEY TURKEY BURGERS

MAKES 4 SERVINGS

1 pound ground turkey

½ cup prepared chutney, divided

½ teaspoon salt

½ teaspoon pepper

⅛ teaspoon hot pepper sauce

½ cup nonfat plain yogurt

1 teaspoon curry powder

4 hamburger buns, split

1 Preheat grill for direct-heat cooking.

2 In medium bowl, combine turkey, ¼ cup chutney, salt, pepper and hot pepper sauce. Shape turkey mixture into 4 burgers, approximately 3½ inches in diameter. Grill turkey burgers 5 to 6 minutes per side until 165°F is reached on meat thermometer and turkey is no longer pink in center.

3 In small bowl, combine yogurt, curry powder and remaining ¼ cup chutney.

4 To serve, place burgers on bottom halves of buns; spoon yogurt mixture over burgers and cover with top halves of buns.

courtesy National Turkey Federation

GREEK CHICKEN BURGERS WITH CUCUMBER YOGURT SAUCE

MAKES 4 SERVINGS

½ cup plus 2 tablespoons plain nonfat Greek yogurt

½ medium cucumber, peeled, seeded and finely chopped

Juice of ½ lemon

3 cloves garlic, minced, divided

2 teaspoons finely chopped fresh mint *or* ½ teaspoon dried mint

⅛ teaspoon salt

⅛ teaspoon ground white pepper

1 pound ground chicken breast

3 ounces reduced-fat crumbled feta cheese

4 large kalamata olives, rinsed, patted dry and minced

1 egg

½ to 1 teaspoon dried oregano

¼ teaspoon black pepper

Mixed baby lettuce and fresh mint leaves (optional)

---

1 Combine yogurt, cucumber, lemon juice, 2 cloves garlic, 2 teaspoons mint, salt and white pepper in medium bowl; mix well. Cover and refrigerate until ready to serve.

2 Combine chicken, cheese, olives, egg, oregano, black pepper and remaining 1 clove garlic in large bowl; mix well. Shape mixture into 4 patties.

3 Spray grill pan with nonstick cooking spray; heat over medium-high heat. Grill patties 5 to 7 minutes per side or until cooked through (165°F).

4 Serve burgers with sauce and mixed greens, if desired. Garnish with mint leaves.

LEMON TURKEY BURGERS

MAKES 4 SERVINGS | PREP TIME 10 MINUTES **COOK TIME** 10 TO 12 MINUTES

1 pound ground turkey

1 cup fresh bread crumbs

¼ cup minced onion

1 egg, lightly beaten

2 tablespoons MRS. DASH® Lemon Pepper Seasoning Blend

1 tablespoon MRS. DASH® Garlic & Herb Seasoning Blend

Nonstick cooking spray

Toasted hamburger buns (optional)

Sweet onion, tomato and cucumber slices (optional)

COMBINE turkey, bread crumbs, onion, egg, MRS. DASH® Lemon Pepper Seasoning Blend and MRS. DASH® Garlic & Herb Seasoning blend in large bowl; mix well. Shape into 4 patties.

PREPARE grill for direct cooking. Spray patties with cooking spray. Grill over medium-high heat 5 to 6 minutes per side or until cooked through (160°F).

SERVE burgers on toasted buns with onion, tomato and cucumber slices, if desired.

FETA AND SPINACH STUFFED TURKEY BURGERS

MAKES 4 SERVINGS

¼ cup cornflake crumbs

¼ cup sliced green onions

3 tablespoons cholesterol-free egg substitute

1 pound 93% lean ground turkey

½ package (10 ounces) frozen chopped spinach, thawed and squeezed dry

⅓ cup crumbled reduced-fat feta cheese

¼ cup chopped black olives

¼ teaspoon black pepper

½ cup chopped fresh tomato

1 Prepare grill for direct cooking. Oil grid.

2 Combine cornflake crumbs, green onions and egg substitute in medium bowl. Add ground turkey; mix well. Pat turkey mixture into 8 (⅜-inch-thick) patties on sheet of waxed paper.

3 Combine spinach, cheese, olives and pepper in small bowl. Place about 2 tablespoons spinach mixture on top of 4 turkey patties. Top with remaining patties; press edges to seal.

4 Grill patties over medium heat 11 to 13 minutes or until cooked through (165°F). Top with chopped tomato.

ENGLISH CHEDDAR TURKEY BURGER

MAKES 4 SERVINGS | PREP TIME 10 MINUTES **COOK TIME** 20 TO 30 MINUTES

1½ tablespoons vegetable oil

1⅓ cups sliced red onions

2 tablespoons white balsamic vinegar

4 BUTTERBALL® Original Seasoned Frozen Turkey Burgers

8 slices (½ ounce each) Cheddar cheese

¼ cup Dijonnaise

1 cup shredded romaine lettuce

4 slices tomatoes

6 tablespoons ketchup

4 English muffins or hamburger buns, split, toasted

1 Heat oil in medium skillet over medium-high heat. Add onions; cook and stir 10 to 15 minutes or until onions are golden brown. Stir in balsamic vinegar until blended; set aside.

2 Cook burgers according to package broiling or grilling directions to an internal temperature of 165°F.

3 When burgers are heated, top each with 2 slices cheese. Broil or grill 1 minute or until cheese is melted.

4 Spread 1 tablespoon Dijonnaise on bottom half of each English muffin. Top each with ¼ cup lettuce, 1 tomato slice, 1 cheese-topped burger, 1½ tablespoons ketchup and ⅓ cup onion mixture. Cover each with top of muffin.

TIP

If Dijonnaise is not available, combine 2 tablespoons each mayonnaise and Dijon-style mustard.

HAWAIIAN TURKEY BURGER

MAKES 4 SERVINGS | PREP TIME 20 MINUTES **TOTAL TIME** LESS THAN 45 MINUTES

4 **BUTTERBALL®** Fresh or Frozen Seasoned Turkey Burger Patties

8 slices Cheddar cheese

4 canned or fresh pineapple slices

Nonstick cooking spray

4 brioche rolls, horizontally split in half (or substitute other type of sandwich bun)

½ cup Dijonnaise

1 cup shredded lettuce

1 cup pickled red onions, drained

3 ounces shaved deli ham

4 tablespoons honey barbecue sauce

1 Prepare grill according to package directions for turkey burgers.

2 Cook burgers according to package grilling directions to an internal temperature of 165°F. Place 2 slices of cheese on each burger during last minute of cooking. Remove burgers from grill; keep warm.

3 Spray pineapple slices with cooking spray. Grill 1 minute per side. Remove from grill.

4 Place rolls, cut side down on grill. Toast 30 to 60 seconds or until light golden brown. Remove from grill.

5 For each burger, spread 1 tablespoon Dijonnaise on each cut surface of roll. Place ¼ cup lettuce on bottom half of roll. Top with 2 tablespoons onion, 1 cooked burger, 1 pineapple slice, and ¾ ounces of the shaved ham. Drizzle ham with 1 tablespoon barbecue sauce. Cover with top of roll. Repeat with remaining ingredients.

VEGGIE-PACKED TURKEY BURGERS

MAKES 4 SERVINGS

1¼ pounds ground turkey

½ cup chopped onion

½ cup shredded zucchini

½ cup shredded carrots

1 teaspoon minced jalapeño pepper

Salt and black pepper

Whole wheat rolls or hamburger buns

Shredded lettuce and tomato slices

1 Prepare grill for direct cooking over medium-heat. Combine turkey, onion, zucchini, carrots and jalapeño pepper in large bowl. Season with salt and black pepper. Shape into 4 patties.

2 Grill, covered, 8 to 10 minutes or until cooked through (160°F), turning halfway through grilling.

3 Serve on rolls with lettuce and tomato slices.

BREAKFAST BURGERS

MAKES 4 SERVINGS

¾ pound extra-lean ground turkey

½ cup minced red bell pepper

½ cup minced green bell pepper

2 teaspoons dried onion flakes

1 teaspoon dried parsley flakes

½ teaspoon black pepper

4 whole wheat English muffins

4 large spinach leaves

4 slices soy cheese

1 Mix turkey, bell peppers, onion flakes, parsley and black pepper in large bowl. Shape mixture into 4 patties; spray with nonstick cooking spray.

2 Cook patties in large nonstick skillet over medium heat 7 minutes or until lightly browned on bottom. Turn and cook 7 minutes more. Add 2 tablespoons water; cover and cook 3 minutes or until cooked through (165°F).

3 Toast English muffins. Place spinach leaf, turkey burger and 1 slice cheese on each muffin half; top with remaining muffin half.

MEATLESS & SEAFOOD BITES

PORTOBELLO MUSHROOM BURGERS

MAKES 4 BURGERS

1¼ teaspoons olive oil, divided

¾ cup thinly sliced shallots

4 large portobello mushrooms, washed, patted dry and stems removed

⅛ teaspoon salt (optional)

⅛ teaspoon black pepper (optional)

2 cloves garlic, minced

¼ cup mayonnaise

2 tablespoons chopped fresh basil

4 whole grain hamburger buns

4 ounces fresh mozzarella cheese, cut into ¼-inch slices

2 jarred roasted red bell peppers, rinsed, patted dry and cut into strips

1 Heat ¼ teaspoon oil in medium saucepan over medium heat. Add shallots; cook and stir 6 to 8 minutes or until golden brown and soft. Set aside.

2 Preheat broiler. Line baking sheet with foil. Drizzle both sides of mushrooms with remaining 1 teaspoon oil; season both with salt and black pepper, if desired.

3 Place mushrooms, cap side down, on foil-lined baking sheet. Sprinkle with garlic. Broil 4 minutes per side.

4 Combine mayonnaise and basil in small bowl.

5 Spread mayonnaise mixture on cut sides of buns. Divide mozzarella slices and shallots evenly among bottom halves of buns; top with mushrooms, roasted peppers and top halves of buns.

CURRIED VEGGIE BURGERS

MAKES 4 SERVINGS

2 eggs

⅓ cup plain yogurt

2 teaspoons vegetarian Worcestershire sauce

2 teaspoons curry powder

½ teaspoon salt

¼ teaspoon ground red pepper

1⅓ cups cooked couscous or brown rice

½ cup finely chopped walnuts

½ cup grated carrots

½ cup minced green onions

⅓ cup plain dry bread crumbs

4 sesame seed hamburger buns

Honey mustard

Thinly sliced cucumber *or* apple

1 Spray grid with nonstick cooking spray; prepare grill for direct cooking.

2 Combine eggs, yogurt, Worcestershire sauce, curry powder, salt and red pepper in large bowl; beat until blended. Stir in couscous, walnuts, carrots, green onions and bread crumbs. Shape into 4 (1-inch-thick) patties.

3 Grill patties over medium-high heat 5 to 6 minutes per side or until done. Serve on buns with mustard and cucumber.

NOTE

Burgers can also be broiled 4 inches from heat source for 5 to 6 minutes per side or until done.

SALMON PATTY BURGERS

MAKES 4 SERVINGS

1 can (about 14 ounces) red salmon, drained

1 egg white

2 tablespoons toasted wheat germ

1 tablespoon dried onion flakes

1 tablespoon capers, drained

½ teaspoon dried thyme

¼ teaspoon black pepper

4 whole wheat buns, split

2 tablespoons Dijon mustard

4 tomato slices

4 thin slices red onion *or* 8 slices dill pickles

4 lettuce leaves

1 Place salmon in medium bowl; mash with fork. Add egg white, wheat germ, onion flakes, capers, thyme and pepper; mix well.

2 Shape mixture into 4 patties; cover and refrigerate 1 hour or until firm.

3 Spray large skillet with nonstick cooking spray. Cook patties over medium heat 5 minutes per side.

4 Spread cut sides of buns with mustard. Place patties on buns; top with tomato and onion slices, lettuce leaves and tops of buns.

TIP

Red salmon is more expensive with a firm texture and deep red color. Pink salmon is less expensive with a light pink color.

CHICKPEA BURGERS

MAKES 4 SERVINGS

1 can (15 ounces) chickpeas, rinsed and drained

⅓ cup chopped carrots

⅓ cup herbed croutons

¼ cup chopped fresh parsley

¼ cup chopped onion

1 egg white

1 teaspoon minced garlic

1 teaspoon grated lemon peel

½ teaspoon black pepper

⅛ teaspoon salt (optional)

4 whole grain hamburger buns

Tomato slices, lettuce leaves and salsa (optional)

1 Place chickpeas, carrots, croutons, parsley, onion, egg white, garlic, lemon peel, pepper and salt, if desired, in food processor; process until blended. Shape mixture into 4 patties.

2 Spray large nonstick skillet with nonstick cooking spray; heat over medium heat. Cook patties 4 to 5 minutes or until bottoms are browned. Spray tops of patties with cooking spray; turn and cook 4 to 5 minutes or until browned.

3 Serve burgers on buns with tomato, lettuce and salsa, if desired.

SALMON BURGER WITH DELICATE TARRAGON AÏOLI SAUCE

MAKES 4 SERVINGS

TARRAGON AÏOLI SAUCE

- ⅓ cup sour cream
- 1½ tablespoons mayonnaise
- 1 tablespoon milk
- ½ teaspoon dried tarragon leaves
- ¼ teaspoon salt
- ⅛ teaspoon black pepper
- 4 lime wedges and cilantro (optional)

BURGER

- 1 vacuum-sealed pouch (6 ounces) pink salmon
- ¼ cup dry bread crumbs
- ⅓ cup chopped green onions
- ¼ cup chopped fresh cilantro
- 2 egg whites
- 2 tablespoons lime juice
- ⅛ teaspoon ground red pepper

1 Combine Tarragon Aïoli Sauce ingredients in small bowl. Refrigerate 10 minutes while making burgers.

2 Combine burger ingredients in medium bowl.

3 Coat large nonstick skillet with nonstick cooking spray and place over medium heat until hot. Spoon equal amounts of salmon mixture into 4 mounds in skillet. Using a flat spatula, flatten each mound. Cook 3 minutes on each side or until golden. Serve with Tarragon Aïoli Sauce along with lime wedges and garnish with cilantro, if desired.

VEGGIE BURGERS

MAKES 8 SERVINGS

3 teaspoons vegetable oil, divided

1 cup sliced mushrooms

1 cup shredded carrots (about 2)

¾ cup chopped onion (about 1 medium)

¾ cup chopped zucchini (about 1 small)

2 cups QUAKER® Oats (quick or old fashioned, uncooked)

1 can (15 ounces) kidney beans, rinsed and drained

1 cup cooked white or brown rice

2 tablespoons soy sauce or ½ teaspoon salt

1 teaspoon minced garlic

⅛ teaspoon black pepper

½ cup chopped fresh cilantro or chives (optional)

Hamburger buns and toppings (optional)

1 Heat 1 teaspoon oil in large nonstick skillet. Add mushrooms, carrots, onion and zucchini; cook over medium-high heat 5 minutes or until vegetables are tender.

2 Transfer vegetables to food processor bowl. Add oats, beans, rice, soy sauce, garlic, pepper and cilantro, if desired. Pulse about 20 seconds or until well blended. Divide into 8 (½-cup) portions. Shape into patties between waxed paper. Refrigerate at least 1 hour or until firm.

3 Heat remaining 2 teaspoons oil in same skillet over medium-high heat. Cook patties 3 to 4 minutes on each side or until golden brown. Serve on buns with toppings, if desired.

FARRO VEGGIE BURGERS

MAKES 6 SERVINGS

1½ cups water

½ cup pearled farro *or* spelt

2 medium potatoes, peeled and quartered

2 to 4 tablespoons canola oil, divided

¾ cup finely chopped green onions

1 cup grated carrots

2 teaspoons grated fresh ginger

2 tablespoons ground almonds

¼ to ¾ teaspoon salt

¼ teaspoon black pepper

½ cup panko bread crumbs

6 whole wheat hamburger buns

Ketchup and mustard (optional)

1 Combine 1½ cups water and farro in medium saucepan; bring to a boil over high heat. Reduce heat to low; partially cover and cook 25 to 30 minutes or until farro is tender. Drain and cool. (If using spelt, use 2 cups of water and cook until tender.)

2 Meanwhile, place potatoes in large saucepan; cover with water. Bring to a boil; reduce heat and simmer 20 minutes or until tender. Cool and mash potatoes; set aside.

3 Heat 1 tablespoon oil in medium skillet over medium-high heat. Add green onions; cook and stir 1 minute. Add carrots and ginger; cover and cook 2 to 3 minutes or until carrots are tender. Transfer to large bowl; cool completely.

4 Add mashed potatoes and farro to carrot mixture. Add almonds, salt and pepper; mix well. Shape mixture into 6 patties. Spread panko on medium plate; coat patties with panko.

5 Heat 1 tablespoon oil in large nonstick skillet over medium heat. Cook patties about 4 minutes per side or until golden brown, adding additional oil as needed. Serve on buns with desired condiments.

NOTE

Farro is a whole grain and belongs to the wheat family. It has a nutty flavor and a chewy bite. It can be used in place of rice in many dishes.

CAPRESE PORTOBELLO BURGERS

MAKES 4 SERVINGS

3 ounces mozzarella cheese, diced

2 plum tomatoes, chopped

2 tablespoons chopped fresh basil

1 tablespoon light balsamic vinaigrette

1 clove garlic, crushed

⅛ teaspoon black pepper

4 portobello mushrooms (about ¾ pound), gills and stems removed

4 whole wheat sandwich thin rounds, toasted

1 Spray grill with nonstick cooking spray and heat over medium-high heat. Meanwhile, combine cheese, tomatoes, basil, vinaigrette, garlic and pepper in small bowl.

2 Grill mushroom caps, stem side down, 5 minutes on each side or until done. Spoon one fourth of tomato mixture into each cap. Cover and grill 3 minutes or until cheese is melted. Serve on sandwich thins.

NOTE

Cooked portobello mushrooms can be frozen and will keep for several months. Store in plastic containers or freezer bags.

MUSTARD GLAZED TOFU BURGERS

MAKES 4 SERVINGS

2 to 3 tablespoons chopped fresh basil

2 to 3 tablespoons honey mustard

2 teaspoons olive oil

2 cloves garlic, minced

1 package (14 ounces) extra firm tofu, pressed*

4 multigrain sandwich thin rounds, split and lightly toasted

½ cup packed arugula or watercress

8 thin slices ripe tomato

Cut tofu in half horizontally; cut in half crosswise to make 4 rectangles. Place it between layers of paper towels. Place a flat heavy object on top; let stand 15 to 30 minutes.

1 Oil grid; prepare grill for direct cooking.

2 Combine basil, mustard, oil and garlic in small bowl; mix well. Spread half of mixture over tofu.

3 Place tofu slices on grid, mustard side down. Spread remaining mustard mixture over tofu; grill, covered, 4 minutes per side or until browned and heated through.

4 Serve in sandwich thins on top of arugula and tomato slices.

SPICY EGGPLANT BURGERS

MAKES 4 SERVINGS

1 eggplant (1¼ pounds), peeled

2 egg whites

½ cup Italian-style panko bread crumbs

3 tablespoons reduced-fat chipotle mayonnaise or regular reduced-fat mayonnaise

4 whole wheat hamburger buns, warmed

1½ cups loosely packed baby spinach

8 thin slices tomato

4 slices pepper Jack cheese

---

1 Preheat oven to 375°F. Spray baking sheet with nonstick cooking spray. Cut 4 slices (½-inch thick) from widest part of eggplant. Beat egg whites in shallow bowl. Place panko on medium plate.

2 Dip eggplant slices in egg whites; dredge in bread crumbs, pressing gently to adhere. Place on prepared baking sheet. Bake 15 minutes or until golden brown; turn and coat with cooking spray. Bake 15 minutes.

3 Spread mayonnaise on bottom halves of buns and top with spinach, tomatoes and eggplant slice. Top with cheese and tops of buns.

FRESH ROCKFISH BURGERS

MAKES 4 SERVINGS

½ pound skinless rockfish or scrod fillet

1 egg white *or* 2 tablespoons cholesterol-free egg substitute

¼ cup plain dry bread crumbs

1 green onion, finely chopped

1 tablespoon finely chopped fresh parsley

2 teaspoons fresh lime juice

1½ teaspoons capers

1 teaspoon Dijon mustard

¼ teaspoon salt

⅛ teaspoon black pepper

4 grilled whole wheat English muffins or hamburger buns

4 leaves green leaf lettuce

8 slices red or yellow tomato

Additional Dijon mustard for serving (optional)

1 Finely chop rockfish and place in medium bowl. Add egg white, bread crumbs, onion, parsley, lime juice, capers, mustard, salt and pepper; gently combine with fork. Shape into 4 patties.

2 Spray heavy grillproof cast iron skillet or griddle with nonstick cooking spray; place on grid over hot coals to heat. Spray tops of burgers with additional cooking spray. Place burgers in hot skillet; grill on covered grill over hot coals 4 to 5 minutes or until burgers are browned on both sides, turning once. Serve on English muffins or buns with lettuce, tomato slices and Dijon mustard, if desired.

PORTOBELLO MUSHROOM BURGER WITH MOZZARELLA

MAKES 4 SERVINGS | PREP TIME 40 MINUTES

⅓ cup olive oil, plus more as needed

2 tablespoons chopped fresh parsley

2 teaspoons red wine vinegar

2 cloves garlic, minced

Salt and black pepper

4 large portobello mushrooms, stems trimmed

4 slices mozzarella cheese

4 thick slices red onion

4 kaiser or rustic rolls, split

2 cups DOLE® Leafy Romaine

4 tablespoons light mayonnaise or other favorite condiment

- Mix oil, parsley, vinegar and garlic in shallow dish; season with salt and pepper. Add mushrooms and turn to coat thoroughly.

- Grill mushrooms over medium-high heat, turning often until just cooked through, 7 to 10 minutes; top with mozzarella and cook 2 minutes more. Lightly brush onion slices with olive oil or any remaining marinade and grill, turning once, about 5 minutes. Toast the rolls, cut side down, on grill.

- Place one mushroom on bottom of each roll. Top each with grilled onion and romaine. Spread mayonnaise on cut side of roll tops and place on burgers. Serve with vegetable chips.

MEATLESS & SEAFOOD BITES

BEANIE BURGERS

MAKES 4 SERVINGS

1 can (about 15 ounces) red kidney beans, rinsed and drained

½ cup chopped onion

⅓ cup quick oats

1 egg

1 tablespoon taco seasoning mix or mild chili powder

½ teaspoon salt

4 slices American cheese

4 whole grain hamburger buns, toasted

4 slices each lettuce and tomato

Salsa, mayonnaise and mustard (optional)

1 Combine beans, onion, oats, egg, taco seasoning mix and salt in food processor. Pulse until mixture is chunky. (Mixture may be made up to 1 day in advance. Cover and refrigerate until needed.)

2 Spray large skillet with nonstick cooking spray; heat over medium heat. Spoon bean mixture into 4 mounds in skillet, spreading into patties with back of spoon.

3 Cook 4 minutes. Turn; top each patty with 1 cheese slice. Cook 4 to 5 minutes. Serve on buns with lettuce, tomato and desired condiments.

LENTIL BURGERS

MAKES 4 SERVINGS

1 can (about 14 ounces) chicken broth

1 cup dried lentils, sorted and rinsed

1 small carrot, grated

¼ cup coarsely chopped mushrooms

1 egg

¼ cup plain dry bread crumbs

3 tablespoons finely chopped onion

2 to 4 cloves garlic, minced

1 teaspoon dried thyme

¼ cup plain fat-free yogurt

¼ cup chopped seeded cucumber

½ teaspoon dried mint

¼ teaspoon dried dill weed

¼ teaspoon black pepper

⅛ teaspoon salt

Dash hot pepper sauce (optional)

Kaiser rolls

1 Bring broth to a boil in medium saucepan over high heat. Stir in lentils; reduce heat to low. Simmer, covered, about 30 minutes or until lentils are tender and liquid is absorbed. Cool to room temperature.

2 Place lentils, carrot and mushrooms in food processor or blender; process until finely chopped but not smooth. (Some whole lentils should still be visible.) Stir in egg, bread crumbs, onion, garlic and thyme. Refrigerate, covered, 2 to 3 hours.

3 Shape lentil mixture into 4 (½-inch-thick) patties. Spray large skillet with nonstick cooking spray; heat over medium heat. Cook patties over medium-low heat about 10 minutes or until browned on both sides.

4 Meanwhile, for sauce, combine yogurt, cucumber, mint, dill, black pepper, salt and hot pepper sauce, if desired, in small bowl. Serve sauce over burgers.

WILD MUSHROOM TOFU BURGERS

MAKES 6 SERVINGS

3 teaspoons olive oil, divided

1 package (8 ounces) cremini mushrooms, roughly chopped

½ medium onion, roughly chopped

1 clove garlic, minced

7 ounces extra firm lite tofu, crumbled and frozen

1 cup old-fashioned oats

⅓ cup finely chopped walnuts

1 egg

½ teaspoon salt

½ teaspoon onion powder

¼ teaspoon dried thyme

6 light multi-grain English muffins, split and toasted

Lettuce, tomato and red onion slices (optional)

Cucumber spears (optional)

1 Heat 1 teaspoon oil in large nonstick skillet over medium heat. Add mushrooms, onion and garlic; cook and stir 10 minutes or until mushrooms have released most of their juices. Remove from heat; cool slightly.

2 Combine mushroom mixture, tofu, oats, walnuts, egg, salt, onion powder and thyme in food processor or blender; process until combined. (Some tofu pieces may remain). Shape mixture into 6 (⅓-cup) patties.

3 Heat 1 teaspoon oil in same skillet over medium-low heat. Working in batches, cook patties 5 minutes per side. Repeat with remaining oil and patties.

4 Serve burgers on English muffins with lettuce, tomato and red onion, if desired. Garnish with cucumber spears.

SLIDERS & MINI BURGERS

SPICY CHEESEBURGER SLIDERS

MAKES 8 SLIDERS

1 pound Ground Beef (96% lean)

9 small whole wheat hamburger buns, split, divided

1 clove garlic, minced

½ teaspoon ground chipotle chili powder

2 slices pepper Jack cheese, cut in quarters

TOPPINGS

Barbecue sauce, lettuce, tomato slices, pickles (optional)

1 Tear one hamburger bun into pieces. Place in food processor or blender container. Cover; pulse on and off, to form fine crumbs.

2 Combine bread crumbs, beef, garlic and chili powder in medium bowl, mixing lightly but thoroughly. Lightly shape into eight ½-inch thick mini patties.

3 Place patties on grill over medium, ash-covered coals. Grill, covered, 8 to 9 minutes (over medium heat on preheated gas grill, 9 to 10 minutes) until instant-read thermometer inserted horizontally into center registers 160°F, turning occasionally. Evenly top with cheese during last minute of grilling.

4 Place burgers on bottoms of remaining eight buns. Top with desired toppings. Close sandwiches.

courtesy The Beef Checkoff

GUACAMOLE SLIDERS

MAKES 12 SMALL BURGERS | PREP TIME 10 MINUTES **START TO FINISH** 20 MINUTES

1 ripe avocado

1 tablespoon ORTEGA® Fire-
Roasted Diced Green Chiles

1 tablespoon chopped cilantro

1 tablespoon lime juice

⅛ teaspoon salt

1 pound lean ground beef

1 tablespoon water

1 cup ORTEGA® Garden Vegetable
Salsa, Medium, divided

12 dinner rolls

CUT avocado in half and remove pit. Scoop out avocado with spoon and place in small bowl. Add chiles, cilantro, lime juice and salt. Gently mash with fork until blended; set aside.

COMBINE beef, water and ½ cup salsa in medium bowl. Form mixture into 12 small round balls. Flatten slightly.

GRILL or pan-fry burgers about 3 minutes. Turn over and flatten with spatula. Cook 4 minutes longer or until desired doneness.

CUT each roll in half. Fill with 1 tablespoon remaining salsa, 1 burger and 1 heaping tablespoon guacamole. Serve immediately.

TIP

Try using a panini press or similar double-sided
grill to cook the sliders even faster.

DUO OF MINI CHEESEBURGERS

MAKES 4 SERVINGS

½ pound ground turkey

1 teaspoon chili powder

½ pound extra-lean ground beef

2 tablespoons minced onion

¼ teaspoon black pepper

2 tablespoons salsa

1 tablespoon hickory-flavored barbecue sauce

4 slices Cheddar or American cheese, halved diagonally

8 small whole wheat dinner rolls, split and lightly toasted

1 Preheat broiler. Line baking sheet with foil; set aside. Combine turkey and chili powder in medium bowl; mix well. Shape into 4 patties about 3 inches in diameter and ½ inch thick. Combine beef, onion and pepper in separate medium bowl; mix well. Shape into 4 patties. Place all patties on prepared baking sheet.

2 Broil patties 4 minutes per side or until no longer pink in center. Spoon salsa over turkey patties and barbecue sauce over beef patties; top all with cheese. Broil 1 minute more or until cheese is melted. Serve in rolls.

TUNA SLIDERS WITH WASABI MAYO

MAKES 24 SLIDERS

⅓ cup light mayonnaise

1 teaspoon wasabi paste

1 teaspoon lemon juice

½ teaspoon grated fresh ginger

3 teaspoons sesame or olive oil

6 (6-ounce) tuna steaks (about 1½ inches thick), cut in half

2 packages (12 ounces each) sweet Hawaiian dinner rolls, split and warmed

12 large lettuce leaves, cut in half

24 small fresh pineapple rings

48 small red onion slices

1 For wasabi mayonnaise, whisk mayonnaise, wasabi paste, lemon juice and ginger in small bowl until smooth and well blended. Set aside.

2 Heat oil in large nonstick skillet over medium-high heat. Cook tuna 2 minutes per side for medium rare or until desired doneness is reached. Cut each piece in half to create 24 pieces.

3 To assemble, spread wasabi mayonnaise on bottoms of rolls. Layer with lettuce, tuna, pineapple, onion and tops of rolls.

MINI BLACK BEAN BURGERS

MAKES 4 SERVINGS

1 small clove garlic, minced

½ cup finely chopped onion

1 cup sliced mushrooms (preferably baby bella)

1 can (about 15 ounces) black beans, drained

¼ cup quick-cooking oats (not instant)

2 tablespoons mayonnaise

½ teaspoon crushed dried thyme

¼ teaspoon salt

¼ teaspoon black pepper

CHIVE SAUCE

2 tablespoons mayonnaise

2 tablespoons plain yogurt

1 tablespoon minced fresh chives

1 Coat 12-inch nonstick skillet with nonstick cooking spray. Add garlic, onion and mushrooms. Cook over medium heat 5 minutes. Remove to blender bowl. Add beans, oats, mayonnaise, thyme, salt and pepper. Process with on/off pulses until mixture is finely minced, but not a paste.

2 Remove black bean mixture from blender and shape into 8 patties, about 2 inches in diameter. Place on large plate covered with waxed paper. Refrigerate 30 minutes.

3 Meanwhile for sauce, in small bowl stir together mayonnaise, yogurt and chives. Set aside.

4 Coat skillet with nonstick cooking spray. Arrange burgers in single layer in skillet. Cook over medium-high heat 5 minutes on first side; turn over gently. Cook an additional 3 to 5 minutes on second side or until browned. Remove from skillet and serve with chive sauce.

NOTE

Handle the burgers carefully. Use a piece of waxed paper to pick up 3 to 4 patties, and flip the paper over in the pan and peel it off.

PIZZA BURGER SLIDERS

MAKES 16 SERVINGS | PREP TIME 15 MINUTES **COOK TIME** 12 MINUTES

2 pounds lean ground beef

1 envelope LIPTON® RECIPE
SECRETS® Onion Soup Mix

½ cup water

16 small slices **or** 2 cups shredded
mozzarella cheese (about
8 ounces)

16 slider-size whole wheat or
regular hamburger buns

2 cups RAGÚ® OLD WORLD
STYLE® Pasta Sauce, heated

1 Combine ground beef, LIPTON® RECIPE SECRETS® Onion Soup Mix and water in
large bowl; shape into 16 patties.

2 Grill or broil until done. Top with cheese, then grill or broil until cheese is melted.
Arrange on buns, then top with RAGÚ® OLD WORLD STYLE® Pasta Sauce.

VARIATION

For regular burgers, simply shape into 8 patties and use 8 slices cheese
and 8 buns.

TIP

These mini burgers are sure to be a hit at your next barbecue.
Shape them, then refrigerate until ready to grill.

OPEN-FACED MINI BLUE CHEESE BURGERS

MAKES 6 SERVINGS (2 PER SERVING)

2 teaspoons olive oil

1 large onion, thinly sliced

¼ teaspoon garlic salt

1 package (20 ounces) lean ground turkey

1½ tablespoons Dijon mustard

¼ cup crumbled blue cheese

4 lettuce leaves, torn into 12 pieces

6 whole wheat mini sandwich thin rounds, split and toasted

1 Heat oil in large nonstick skillet over medium-high heat. Add onion; cook and stir 3 minutes. Reduce heat to medium; cook onion 10 minutes or until golden brown, stirring frequently.

2 Meanwhile, mix garlic salt into ground turkey. Shape turkey into 12 (¼-inch-thick) patties.

3 Spray large skillet with nonstick cooking spray; heat over medium heat. Cook burgers in batches 3 minutes on each side or until cooked through.

4 Combine mustard and blue cheese in small bowl. Place 1 lettuce leaf on bottom of each sandwich thin; top with burger, blue cheese mixture and onions.

RAMEN SLIDERS

MAKES 6 SERVINGS (2 PER SERVING)

BUNS

- 1 tablespoon sesame seeds
- 2 packages (3 ounces each) beef-flavored ramen noodles*
- 2 eggs
- ¼ teaspoon garlic powder

BURGERS

- 1 pound ground beef
- ½ teaspoon salt
- ½ teaspoon black pepper
- ½ teaspoon garlic powder
- 1 tablespoon vegetable oil

TOPPINGS

- 3 slices American cheese, cut into 4 squares each
- 12 lettuce leaves
- 2 ripe medium plum tomatoes
- 12 hamburger dill pickle slices
- ¼ cup thinly sliced red onion
  Ketchup and mustard to taste

Discard 1 seasoning packet.

TO MAKE BUNS

1 Preheat oven to 350°F. Lightly coat 2 nonstick 12-cup muffin tin pans with nonstick cooking spray. Spoon ⅛ teaspoon sesame seeds in each cup. Set aside.

2 Break each layer of ramen noodles into 4 pieces. Cook noodles according to package directions; rinse and drain under cold water, shaking off excess liquid and blotting on paper towels to dry.

3 Whisk eggs, 1 seasoning packet and ¼ teaspoon garlic powder in large bowl until smooth. Add noodles; toss until well coated. Place equal amounts of noodle mixture in each of the 24 sections of prepared pans. Bake 10 minutes or until set. Remove from oven; flip over in pan, cool completely while sitting in pan.

TO MAKE BURGERS

4 Shape beef into 12 (2½-inch) patties. Combine salt, pepper and ½ teaspoon garlic powder in small bowl. Sprinkle evenly over both sides of patties.

5 Heat oil in large nonstick skillet over medium-high heat. Working in 2 batches, cook patties 2 minutes on each side. Remove from heat, top each with a cheese square; set aside. Repeat with remaining patties and cheese.

TO ASSEMBLE

6 Place half of "buns" on serving platter. Top with lettuce, patties, choice of toppings and "bun" tops.

TWO-BITE BURGERS

MAKES 8 BURGERS

1 pound Ground Beef (96% lean)

9 whole wheat small hamburger or slider buns, split, divided

¼ cup minced onion

1 egg white

2 cloves garlic, minced

½ teaspoon salt

⅛ teaspoon pepper

TOPPING VARIATIONS

Mango-Pineapple Salsa, Spicy Caramelized Onions or Creamy Yogurt-Feta Sauce (recipes follow)

---

1 Tear one hamburger bun into pieces. Place in food processor or blender container. Cover; pulse on and off, to form fine crumbs.

2 Combine Ground Beef, ½ cup bread crumbs, onion, egg white, garlic, salt and pepper in medium bowl, mixing lightly but thoroughly. Lightly shape into eight ½-inch thick mini patties.

3 Place patties on grid over medium, ash-covered coals. Grill, covered, 8 to 9 minutes (over medium heat on preheated gas grill, 9 to 10 minutes) until instant-read thermometer inserted horizontally into center registers 160°F, turning occasionally. About 1½ minutes before burgers are done, place rolls, cut sides down, on grid. Grill until lightly toasted.

4 Serve burgers in buns with Topping Variation(s), as desired. Close sandwiches.

SERVING SUGGESTION

Serve burgers with fresh or pickled vegetables.

COOK'S TIPS

To broil burgers, preheat broiler. Place burgers on rack in broiler pan so surface of beef is 2 to 3 inches from heat element. Broil 9 to 10 minutes to medium (160°F) doneness, turning the burgers once. Place buns, cut sides up, on broiler pan so surface is 2 to 3 inches from heat element. Broil 45 to 60 seconds or until lightly toasted.

Cooking times are for fresh or thoroughly thawed Ground Beef. Color is not a reliable indicator of Ground Beef doneness.

courtesy The Beef Checkoff

MANGO-PINEAPPLE SALSA

Combine ½ cup finely diced ripe mango or ½ cup finely diced drained jarred ripe mango, ⅓ cup finely chopped fresh pineapple or ⅓ cup drained canned crushed pineapple, ¼ cup finely chopped tomato, 1 to 2 tablespoons finely chopped jalapeño pepper, 1 tablespoon finely chopped fresh mint, 1 tablespoon fresh lime juice and ¼ teaspoon salt in small bowl. Refrigerate until ready to use.
Makes 1 cup.

SPICY CARAMELIZED ONIONS

Heat 1 tablespoon olive oil in large nonstick skillet over medium heat until hot. Add 3 cups thinly sliced yellow onions and 2 to 3 medium thinly sliced red or green jalapeño peppers or 6 thinly sliced baby sweet red bell peppers. Cook 5 minutes, stirring occasionally. Reduce heat to medium-low; stir in ½ teaspoon cumin. Cook 15 to 18 minutes or until onions are very tender and golden brown, stirring frequently. Season with salt, as desired. *Makes 1½ cups.*

CREAMY YOGURT-FETA SAUCE

Combine ½ cup reduced-fat or nonfat plain or Greek yogurt, ¼ cup reduced-fat or regular crumbled feta cheese, 2 tablespoons minced onion and 1 teaspoon chopped fresh oregano or ¼ teaspoon dried oregano leaves in small bowl. Season with salt and pepper, as desired. Refrigerate until ready to use.
Makes ¾ cup.

SLIDERS & MINI BURGERS

TASTE OF DOLE® ISLAND PORK SLIDERS

MAKES 12 SERVINGS | PREP TIME 35 MINUTES **CHILL TIME** 30 MINUTES **COOK TIME** 10 MINUTES

¾ cup mayonnaise with olive oil

1 can (20 oz.) DOLE® Pineapple Tidbits, drained, reserved juice, divided

2 garlic cloves, finely chopped, divided

¾ cup DOLE® Frozen Mango Chunks, partially thawed, divided

2 teaspoons ground ginger, divided

Coarse sea salt and ground black pepper, to taste

¾ cup jicama, julienned

⅔ cup fresh cilantro, coarsely chopped, divided

2 pounds lean ground pork

1 teaspoon ground cumin

½ teaspoon red pepper flakes

½ cup Island teriyaki sauce or regular teriyaki sauce, divided

12 Hawaiian sweet rolls, lightly toasted

- Combine mayonnaise, ⅓ cup pineapple tidbits, 1 clove garlic, ½ cup mango chunks and 1 teaspoon ground ginger in blender or food processor. Cover; blend until smooth. Season with salt and ground black pepper to taste.

- Chop finely remaining pineapple tidbits and mangoes; set aside. Stir together 1 cup pineapple tidbits, jicama and ½ cup cilantro in medium bowl. Season with salt and ground black pepper, to taste.

- Combine pork, reserved pineapple juice, ¼ cup pineapple tidbits, remaining mango, ground cumin, red pepper flakes, ¼ cup teriyaki sauce and 1½ teaspoons sea salt. Add remaining garlic, ginger and cilantro until just mixed. Divide mixture into 12 equal portions and shape into patties about 3½-inches wide. Cover; refrigerate until ready to cook.

- Lightly coat large nonstick skillet with vegetable oil, heat over medium-high heat. Place patties in skillet and cook 3 to 5 minutes on each side turning once until pork is fully cooked (145°F.). During last few minutes of cooking baste patties equally with remaining teriyaki sauce.

- Assemble sliders; spread cut sides of buns with equal portions of ginger pineapple mango mayonnaise. On each bottom, place a patty and equal portions of pineapple jicama salsa. Add bun tops and serve.

WAFFLED BURGER SLIDERS

MAKES 8 SLIDERS

½ **pound lean ground beef**

½ **teaspoon salt**

Black pepper

8 **slider buns** *or* **4 slices bread, cut into quarters**

1 **tablespoon butter, melted**

Desired toppings (lettuce, tomatoes, cheese, pickles, ketchup)

1 Combine beef, salt and pepper in large bowl. Divide into 8 small patties; set aside.

2 Heat waffle maker to medium. Brush buns with melted butter; set aside.

3 Place 4 patties at a time in waffle maker. Cook, about 3 minutes, or until cooked through. Place 1 patty in each bun, adding desired toppings.

HERBED CHICKEN DIJON SLIDERS

MAKES 12 SLIDERS

1 pound ground chicken

⅓ cup chopped green onions

2 tablespoons Worcestershire sauce

1½ to 2 teaspoons chopped fresh thyme

1 clove garlic, minced

12 whole wheat dinner rolls, cut in half

¼ cup Dijon mustard

2 cups mixed salad greens

1 tomato, cut into 12 thin slices

1 Mix chicken, green onions, Worcestershire sauce, thyme and garlic in large bowl. Shape into 12 (½-inch-thick) patties.

2 Spray large skillet with nonstick cooking spray; heat over medium heat. Cook patties 4 to 5 minutes on each side or until cooked through (165°F).

3 Spread bottom halves of buns with 1 teaspoon Dijon mustard. Top burgers with salad greens, tomato slices and top halves of buns.

CHICKEN NUGGET SLIDERS

MAKES 4 SERVINGS | PREP TIME 20 MINUTES

- ¼ cup HELLMANN'S® or BEST FOODS® Real Mayonnaise
- 2 tablespoons ketchup
- 12 party-size potato rolls, split
- 12 frozen or refrigerated chicken nuggets*, cooked according to package directions

- 3 slices Cheddar or muenster cheese, cut into quarters
- 3 slices bacon, crisp-cooked and broken into 12 pieces
- 12 small iceberg lettuce leaves

*Try with your favorite homemade chicken nugget recipe or chicken tenders cut into pieces.

Combine HELLMANN'S® or BEST FOODS® Real Mayonnaise with ketchup in small bowl; spread on bottom of rolls. Top with remaining ingredients.

BUFFALO SLIDERS

MAKES 6 SERVINGS | PREP TIME 5 MINUTES **COOK TIME** 6 MINUTES

1½ pounds ground beef
½ cup finely chopped bell pepper
3 tablespoons any flavor
   FRANK'S® RedHot® Buffalo
   Wings Sauce

12 mini slider buns or dinner rolls
   Lettuce and shredded cheese

MIX beef, bell pepper and **FRANK'S RedHot** Buffalo Wings Sauce; shape into 12 mini patties.

GRILL or broil sliders until desired doneness, turning once.

SERVE sliders on rolls with lettuce and cheese.

SIDES & SWEETS

BEST 'CUE COLE SLAW

MAKES 6 TO 8 SERVINGS

⅓ cup dill pickle relish

⅓ cup vegetable oil

3 tablespoons lime juice

2 tablespoons honey

1 teaspoon salt

1 teaspoon ground cumin

1 teaspoon ground red pepper

1 teaspoon black pepper

1 small head green cabbage, very thinly sliced

2 large carrots, shredded

1 bunch green onions, sliced

5 radishes, sliced

1 Combine relish, oil, lime juice, honey, salt, cumin, red pepper and black pepper in large bowl. Add cabbage, carrots, green onions and radishes; stir until well combined.

2 Chill at least 1 hour before serving.

VARIATION

For a sweeter taste, add slivered apples instead of the dill pickle relish.

FRUITY WILD RICE SALAD

MAKES 6 SERVINGS

1¾ cups water

1 package (about 6 ounces) long grain and wild rice mix (fast cook recipe)

½ cup finely chopped dried apricots

⅓ cup coarsely chopped hazelnuts

6 tablespoons chopped fresh Italian parsley

¼ teaspoon curry powder

¼ teaspoon ground cumin

¼ teaspoon black pepper

Pinch ground red pepper

1½ cups finely shredded or chopped red cabbage

1½ tablespoons white wine vinegar

1 tablespoon honey

½ teaspoon salt

1½ tablespoons vegetable oil

1 Combine water, rice mix, apricots, hazelnuts, parsley, curry powder, cumin, black pepper and red pepper in large saucepan. Bring to a boil. Cover and reduce heat to low. Simmer 10 minutes or until rice is tender. Remove from heat. Let stand 5 minutes.

2 Transfer to large bowl; cool to room temperature. Stir in red cabbage.

3 Combine vinegar, honey and salt in small bowl, stirring until salt dissolves. Whisk in oil. Pour over salad; toss to coat.

GRILLED POTATO SALAD

MAKES 4 SERVINGS

¼ cup country-style Dijon mustard

2 tablespoons chopped fresh dill

1 tablespoon white wine vinegar
   or apple cider vinegar

1½ teaspoons salt, divided

¼ teaspoon black pepper

5 tablespoons olive oil, divided

8 cups water

2 pounds small red potatoes

1 green onion, thinly sliced

1 Prepare grill for direct cooking.

2 Whisk mustard, dill, vinegar, ½ teaspoon salt and pepper in measuring cup. Gradually whisk in 3 tablespoons oil. Set aside.

3 Bring water and remaining 1 teaspoon salt to a boil in large saucepan over medium-high heat. Cut potatoes into ½-inch slices. Add potatoes to saucepan; boil 5 minutes. Drain; return potatoes to saucepan. Drizzle with remaining 2 tablespoons oil; toss lightly.

4 Spray one side of large foil sheet with nonstick cooking spray. Transfer potatoes to foil; fold into packet. Place potato packet on grid. Grill 10 minutes or until potatoes are tender. Transfer potatoes to serving bowl. Sprinkle with green onion. Add dressing and toss gently to coat. Serve warm.

POTATO AND BLUE CHEESE SALAD

MAKES 4 TO 6 SERVINGS

8 new or fingerling potatoes (about 1 pound), scrubbed

½ teaspoon salt

½ cup shredded radicchio

¼ cup pitted kalamata or niçoise olives, halved

¼ cup (1 ounce) crumbled blue or Gorgonzola cheese

2½ tablespoons olive oil

1 teaspoon white wine vinegar

1 teaspoon Dijon mustard

¼ teaspoon black pepper

1 Place potatoes and salt in medium saucepan; add water to cover. Bring to a boil; cook about 20 to 25 minutes or until potatoes are tender. Drain well; cut into bite-size pieces.

2 Combine potatoes, radicchio, olives and cheese in large bowl. Whisk oil, vinegar, mustard and pepper in small bowl. Pour over potato mixture; stir gently to coat. Let stand 30 minutes to allow flavors to blend. Serve at room temperature.

VARIATION

Replace cheese with feta cheese, and use sun-dried tomatoes and fresh basil instead of radicchio.

SWEET POTATO & FRUIT SALAD

MAKES 4 TO 6 SERVINGS

2 sweet potatoes (8 ounces)

1 Granny Smith apple, unpeeled and chopped

¼ cup chopped celery

1 container (6 ounces) plain fat-free yogurt

2 tablespoons orange juice

½ to 1 teaspoon grated fresh ginger

½ teaspoon curry powder

⅛ teaspoon salt

½ cup cinnamon-coated nuts, divided

¼ cup drained mandarin oranges

1 Pierce sweet potatoes in several places with fork and place on microwavable dish. Cover loosely with plastic wrap. Microwave on HIGH 6 to 7 minutes, turning over halfway through cooking time. Cool completely.

2 Peel sweet potatoes and cut into 1-inch pieces. Combine sweet potatoes, apple and celery in large bowl.

3 Combine yogurt, orange juice, ginger, curry powder and salt in small bowl. Add to sweet potato mixture; toss to coat. Add half of nuts; stir gently. Top with remaining nuts and oranges. Refrigerate until ready to serve.

VARIATION

Any type of flavored nut will work great, including honey-roasted or praline-coated varieties.

TIP

Add some chopped jalapeño pepper to spice it up.

HOT AND SPICY FRUIT SALAD

MAKES 6 SERVINGS

⅓ cup orange juice

3 tablespoons lime juice

3 tablespoons minced fresh mint, basil or cilantro

2 jalapeño peppers,* seeded, minced

1 tablespoon honey

½ small honeydew melon, cut into cubes

1 ripe large papaya, peeled, seeded, cubed

1 pint strawberries, stemmed, halved

1 can (8 ounces) pineapple chunks, drained

*Jalapeño peppers can sting and irritate the skin, so wear rubber gloves when handling peppers and do not touch your eyes.

1 Blend orange juice, lime juice, mint, jalapeño peppers and honey in small bowl.

2 Combine melon, papaya, strawberries and pineapple in large bowl. Pour orange juice mixture over fruit; toss gently until well blended.

3 Serve immediately or cover and refrigerate up to 3 hours. Garnish with fresh mint, if desired.

CREAMY AND CRUNCHY COLESLAW

MAKES 6 SERVINGS

1 tablespoon vegetable oil

2 packages (3 ounces each) ramen noodles, any flavor*

½ cup sliced almonds

½ cup mayonnaise

¼ cup rice wine vinegar

2 teaspoons honey

1 teaspoon sesame oil

1 teaspoon soy sauce

Hot pepper sauce, to taste

2 cups shredded napa cabbage

½ cup sliced green onions

Discard seasoning packets.

1 Heat vegetable oil in medium skillet over medium heat. Crush half of one package noodles into skillet; cook and stir 2 minutes. Add almonds; cook and stir 2 minutes or until golden brown. Transfer to plate.

2 Bring water to a boil in medium saucepan over medium-high heat. Add remaining noodles; cook 2 minutes. Drain and rinse with cold water.

3 Combine mayonnaise, vinegar, honey, sesame oil, soy sauce and hot pepper sauce in large bowl; mix well. Add boiled noodles, cabbage and green onions; toss to coat. Top with toasted noodles and almonds just before serving.

MANDARIN SALAD

MAKES 4 SERVINGS

⅓ cup olive oil

2 tablespoons cider vinegar

2 teaspoons honey

2 teaspoons dried tarragon

½ teaspoon dry mustard

¼ teaspoon salt

⅛ teaspoon black pepper

1 can (11 ounces) mandarin oranges, drained, and 1 tablespoon juice reserved

4 cups chopped romaine lettuce

1 package (3 ounces) ramen noodles, any flavor, lightly crumbled*

½ cup toasted pecans, coarsely chopped**

¼ cup chopped red onion

*Discard seasoning packet.

**To toast pecans, spread in single layer in small heavy skillet. Cook over medium heat 1 to 2 minutes or until nuts are lightly browned, stirring frequently. Remove from skillet immediately. Cool before using.*

1 Whisk oil, vinegar, honey, tarragon, mustard, salt, pepper and reserved mandarin orange juice in large bowl.

2 Add lettuce, oranges, crumbled noodles, pecans and onion to dressing; toss to combine.

CREAMY COLESLAW

MAKES 8 SERVINGS

½ cup light mayonnaise

½ cup low-fat buttermilk

2 teaspoons sugar

1 teaspoon celery seed

1 teaspoon fresh lime juice

½ teaspoon chili powder

3 cups shredded coleslaw mix

1 cup shredded carrots

¼ cup finely chopped red onion

Whisk mayonnaise, buttermilk, sugar, celery seed, lime juice and chili powder in large bowl until smooth and well blended. Add coleslaw mix, carrots and onion; toss to coat evenly. Cover and refrigerate at least 2 hours before serving.

CRANBERRY FRUIT SALAD

MAKES 8 SERVINGS

2 large navel oranges

2 large pink grapefruit

1 cup seedless grapes

2 kiwi, peeled, halved lengthwise and sliced into bite-size pieces (½ cup)

¾ cup light cranberry juice cocktail

2 tablespoons dried cranberries

1 Grate orange peel to measure 1 teaspoon. Peel oranges and grapefruit. Cut fruit into segments over large bowl, leaving behind white pith. Squeeze pith and peels over bowl to extract any remaining juice.

2 Stir in grapes, kiwi, cranberry juice, cranberries and grated orange peel. Serve immediately.

MINI DESSERT BURGERS

MAKES 24 SERVINGS | PREP TIME 30 MINUTES **COOKING TIME** 1 MINUTE **COOLING TIME** 10 MINUTES

1 box (12 ounces) vanilla wafer cookies,* *divided*

½ cup powdered sugar

¼ teaspoon salt

¾ cup NESTLÉ® TOLL HOUSE® Semi-Sweet Chocolate Morsels

⅓ cup milk

½ cup sweetened flaked coconut

½ teaspoon water

3 drops green food coloring

Red and yellow decorating gels (for ketchup and mustard)

1 teaspoon melted butter (optional)

1 tablespoon sesame seeds (optional)

A 12-ounce box of vanilla wafers contains about 88 wafers.

RESERVE 48 wafers for bun tops and bottoms.

PLACE remaining wafers in large resealable bag. Crush into small pieces using a rolling pin. Combine wafer crumbs (about 1½ cups) with powdered sugar and salt in medium bowl.

MICROWAVE morsels and milk in medium, uncovered, microwave-safe bowl on HIGH (100%) power for 45 seconds; STIR. If necessary, microwave at additional 10- to 15-second intervals, stirring just until smooth.

POUR chocolate mixture into wafer mixture; stir until combined. Cool for 10 minutes. Line baking sheet with wax paper. Roll mixture into 24, 1-inch (about 1 tablespoonful each) balls. Place each ball on prepared sheet; flatten slightly to form burger patties.

COMBINE coconut, water and green food coloring in small, resealable plastic bag. Seal bag and shake to coat evenly with color.

TO ASSEMBLE

PLACE 24 wafers, rounded side down on prepared baking sheet. Top each wafer with 1 burger patty. Top each burger patty with 1 teaspoon colored coconut. Squeeze decorating gels on top of coconut. Top with remaining wafers. Brush tops of wafers with melted butter and sprinkle with sesame seeds, if desired.

CHEESEBURGERS!

Cut apricot fruit rollups into small ½-inch squares to create cheese for the mini burgers.

GRILLED PINEAPPLE WITH ICE CREAM AND CHOCOLATE

MAKES 4 SERVINGS

2 tablespoons cinnamon-sugar*

¼ teaspoon allspice

8 (¾-inch-thick) slices fresh pineapple

Vanilla ice cream or any flavor

Chocolate, fudge, butterscotch or caramel sauce

To make cinnamon-sugar, combine 2 tablespoons sugar with 1 teaspoon ground cinnamon.

1 Combine cinnamon-sugar with allspice in small bowl. Sprinkle pineapple slices with spice mixture. Place onto medium-low grill and grill until tender. Turn as needed, until golden brown, about 7 minutes.

2 Place pineapple slices on plates. Top pineapple with ice cream and drizzle with chocolate sauce that has been heated in microwave for about 15 seconds.

GRILLED PEACHES WITH NUTMEG PASTRY CREAM

MAKES 4 SERVINGS

4 peaches, halved

2 tablespoons cinnamon-sugar*

3 egg yolks

⅓ cup sugar

2 tablespoons all-purpose flour

Pinch salt

1¼ cups whole milk

1 teaspoon vanilla

⅛ teaspoon ground nutmeg

2 tablespoons butter

Whipped cream (optional)

To make cinnamon-sugar, combine 2 tablespoons sugar with 1 teaspoon ground cinnamon.

1 Prepare grill for direct cooking. Sprinkle peach halves with cinnamon-sugar. Grill over medium-low heat just until tender and slightly golden brown. (Peaches should still be firm and hold shape.) Set aside.

2 Combine egg yolks, sugar, flour and salt in medium bowl; stir until well blended.

3 Bring milk, vanilla and nutmeg to a boil in medium saucepan over medium-low heat. Whisking constantly, slowly add ¼ cup hot milk mixture to egg yolk mixture.

4 Add egg yolk mixture to milk mixture in saucepan; cook, whisking constantly, until thickened. Remove from heat and add butter; whisk until well blended.

5 Spoon sauce onto dessert plates; arrange peach halves on top of sauce. Serve with whipped cream, if desired.

GRILLED BANANA SPLITS

MAKES 2 SERVINGS

2 large ripe firm bananas

½ teaspoon melted butter

2 tablespoons chocolate syrup

½ teaspoon orange liqueur (optional)

1 cup vanilla ice cream

2 tablespoons sliced almonds, toasted*

To toast almonds, spread in single layer on baking sheet. Bake in preheated 350°F oven 8 to 10 minutes or until golden brown, stirring frequently.

1 Spray grid with nonstick cooking spray. Prepare grill for direct cooking.

2 Cut unpeeled bananas lengthwise; brush melted butter over cut sides. Grill bananas, cut side down, over medium-hot coals 2 minutes or until lightly browned; turn. Grill 2 minutes or until tender.

3 Combine syrup and liqueur, if desired, in small bowl.

4 Cut bananas in half crosswise; carefully remove peel. Place banana slices in each bowl; top with ice cream, chocolate syrup and almonds; serve immediately.

GRILLED PINEAPPLE WITH CARAMEL DIPPING SAUCE

MAKES 4 SERVINGS

25 unwrapped caramels

⅓ cup half-and-half

¼ teaspoon rum flavoring

1 ripe pineapple, trimmed and sliced into 8 (½-inch) slices

1. Place unwrapped caramels, half-and-half and flavoring in small saucepan. Cook over low to medium-low heat, stirring until sauce is thick and smooth. Keep warm until ready to serve.

2. Place pineapple on grid over medium heat. Grill 10 to 12 minutes or until pineapple softens and turns deeper yellow in color, turning once.

3. Place pineapple on cutting board; cut into bite-size pieces. Discard core pieces. Serve pineapple with caramel sauce for dipping or drizzle over pineapple before serving.

INDEX

ACKNOWLEDGEMENTS

**The publisher would like to thank the following companies and organizations
for the use of their recipes and photographs in this publication.**

The Beef Checkoff
Butterball® Turkey
Campbell Soup Company
Dole Food Company, Inc.
Heinz North America
®Johnsonville Sausage, LLC
Mrs. Dash®, A Division of B&G Foods North America, Inc.
National Pork Board
National Turkey Federation
Nestlé USA
Ortega®, A Division of B&G Foods North America, Inc.
Pinnacle Foods
The Quaker® Oatmeal Kitchens
Reckitt Benckiser LLC
Unilever

METRIC CONVERSION CHART

VOLUME MEASUREMENTS (dry)

1/8 teaspoon = 0.5 mL
1/4 teaspoon = 1 mL
1/2 teaspoon = 2 mL
3/4 teaspoon = 4 mL
1 teaspoon = 5 mL
1 tablespoon = 15 mL
2 tablespoons = 30 mL
1/4 cup = 60 mL
1/3 cup = 75 mL
1/2 cup = 125 mL
2/3 cup = 150 mL
3/4 cup = 175 mL
1 cup = 250 mL
2 cups = 1 pint = 500 mL
3 cups = 750 mL
4 cups = 1 quart = 1 L

VOLUME MEASUREMENTS (fluid)

1 fluid ounce (2 tablespoons) = 30 mL
4 fluid ounces (1/2 cup) = 125 mL
8 fluid ounces (1 cup) = 250 mL
12 fluid ounces (1 1/2 cups) = 375 mL
16 fluid ounces (2 cups) = 500 mL

WEIGHTS (mass)

1/2 ounce = 15 g
1 ounce = 30 g
3 ounces = 90 g
4 ounces = 120 g
8 ounces = 225 g
10 ounces = 285 g
12 ounces = 360 g
16 ounces = 1 pound = 450 g

DIMENSIONS

1/16 inch = 2 mm
1/8 inch = 3 mm
1/4 inch = 6 mm
1/2 inch = 1.5 cm
3/4 inch = 2 cm
1 inch = 2.5 cm

OVEN TEMPERATURES

250°F = 120°C
275°F = 140°C
300°F = 150°C
325°F = 160°C
350°F = 180°C
375°F = 190°C
400°F = 200°C
425°F = 220°C
450°F = 230°C

BAKING PAN SIZES

Utensil	Size in Inches/Quarts	Metric Volume	Size in Centimeters
Baking or Cake Pan (square or rectangular)	8×8×2	2 L	20×20×5
	9×9×2	2.5 L	23×23×5
	12×8×2	3 L	30×20×5
	13×9×2	3.5 L	33×23×5
Loaf Pan	8×4×3	1.5 L	20×10×7
	9×5×3	2 L	23×13×7
Round Layer Cake Pan	8×1½	1.2 L	20×4
	9×1½	1.5 L	23×4
Pie Plate	8×1¼	750 mL	20×3
	9×1¼	1 L	23×3
Baking Dish or Casserole	1 quart	1 L	—
	1½ quart	1.5 L	—
	2 quart	2 L	—